文
景
———
Horizon

湖岸®

Hu'an

当我环顾四周，却始终无法找到我的梦想之车，我决定亲手打造一台。

——费利·保时捷

［德］斯特凡·博格纳 ［德］扬·卡尔·贝德克尔 著 丁伯骏 译

Stefan Bogner · Jan Karl Baedeker

Porsche Unseen
Design Studies

见所未见
保时捷的未来设计

保时捷设计工作室从未发布过的概念车

Unpublished Concept Cars from the Porsche Design Studios

EDITION PORSCHE MUSEUM

上海人民出版社

"多年以来,
祖文豪森与魏斯阿赫一直被称作
汽车工业中的'硅谷'。"

——毛迈恪

"For many years the
Silicon Valley for the
automobile industry has
been in Zuffenhausen
and Weissach."

Michael Mauer

来自未来的记忆
Future Memories

眼界与革新：毛迈恪与保时捷的设计文化

Vision and Innovation: Michael Mauer and the Porsche Design Culture

尽管毛迈恪的正式职位是保时捷的首席设计师，但他还在保时捷魏斯阿赫研发中心长期掌管一项秘密的"时光旅行项目"。每天早晨，他和团队成员都会穿过重重安检屏障，在咖啡机前注入充满灵感与创意的燃料，然后将当下一切抛掷脑后，踏上一段穿越到未来的奇妙旅程。当然，他们会在下班之后重新回到现实，只不过脑海中多出了来自2030、2040甚至2050年的新点子。事实上，保时捷的设计室是一个巨大的创意工坊，一个革新的温室，这里甚至鼓励和追求最天马行空的创意。这支团队总是会留心那些不经意擦出的创意火花、那些独创性的想法以及那些对于设计未来汽车来说至关重要的思考。

保时捷向来以其精湛的跑车与独立的造车精神闻名于世。保时捷911如今依然屹立于时代的潮头，靠的便是70多年来先锋般的后置发动机布局、由此带来的独特车身比例以及自成一派的设计风格。在赛场上，保时捷也自成一派，依靠巧妙的工程设计而非绝对速度的设计理念让保时捷获得了超过三万个全场及组别冠军。除此之外，保时捷还凭借新晋家族成员 Taycan 跻身了纯电动跑车领域。以上谈到的所有保时捷车，是否有灵魂上的共鸣之处呢？保时捷品牌持续成功的秘诀是什么？自从伟大的设计师费迪南德·保时捷的时代以来，打破常规、质疑当下、革新自我便刻在了这个品牌的DNA中。这些至关重要的元素不仅存在于保时捷的每一款量产车中，更包含在设计师构想的每

Michael Mauer's official title may be Head of Design at Porsche – but secretly he is leading a huge time travel project at the Development Center in Weissach. Every morning he and his design team pass through the high security locks, fill up with creative rocket fuel at the espresso machine and leave the present behind to embark on a journey of the mind into the world of tomorrow. They return after work armed with fresh new ideas from 2030, 2040 or 2050. The fact is that, Porsche's design studio is a huge ideas workshop, an innovative think tank where even the craziest visions are encouraged and pursued. The team is always on the lookout for the next ingenious design, a decisive idea or a further step on the way to developing the automobile of the future.

Porsche is famous for its sports cars and for its independence of spirit. The Porsche 911 is still successfully swimming against the tide to this day – as a pioneering rear-engined vehicle, design icon and symbol of an idea that is more than 70 years old. Porsche has also marched to the beat of its own drum in the racing world, relying on intelligent solutions instead of sheer performance and writing history with more than 30,000 overall and class victories by works racing drivers and privateers. The Porsche Taycan recently ventured into new territory as the brand's first fully electric production sports car. But what are the essential characteristics and qualities that all Porsches have in common? What is the secret of the brand's continued success? Since the days of the great designer Ferdinand Porsche, the name seems to have been synonymous with an ability to think outside of the box, questioning the status quo and constantly reinventing oneself. This is not only evident in the production models with which Porsche launched its global

一个灵感，绘制的每一张手稿和搭建的每一个模型之中。不过，这些组成品牌进化的重要部分，往往被尘封在设计室的最深处。

这是保时捷历史上的第一次，作为设计部门老大的毛迈恪将魏斯阿赫保时捷设计工作室的大门敞开，让更多人知道其中的秘密。经过他的允许，我们见到了在他指导下过去近20年中保时捷最大胆、最梦幻、最惊人的设计作品。本书旨在为读者创造一个奇幻的"平行宇宙"，在这里你可以见到平日里从未想象过的、最出乎意料的保时捷。甚至在本书创作的过程中，我们都要时不时地提醒自己，这些车并不是我们凭空臆想出来的，而真的是由保时捷的设计师们亲手打造，例如可以立刻上路飞驰的摩登版911 Safari越野车，经典的保时捷904在当代的重置版，乃至作为Taycan设计探索的四门超级跑车模型等等。那天晚上，如果设计主管用友好且坚定的语气要求我们盯着一个可以抹去记忆的小设备，让我们忘掉所见的一切，我们也不会觉得奇怪。

为什么这些车从未被投入量产？这个问题对毛迈恪来说并不重要，因为不是每一个对品牌有前瞻作用的设计都需要被量产。对于他和他的团队来说，这些试验性质的作品更需要为保时捷未来的产品打开视野、探寻方向、定下基调，有些想法甚至仅仅停留在草稿纸上或电脑中。

triumph, but also in the countless ideas, sketches, models, studies and prototypes that are important parts of the brand evolution, but that usually remain hidden behind studio doors.

For the first time in the recent history of Porsche, design boss Michael Mauer has now opened the doors to the secret archives of the Porsche Design Studio in Weissach. In doing so, he has granted us a glimpse of many of the courageous, fascinating and surprising concept cars that have been created under his direction over almost two decades. This book aims to take our readers on a fascinating journey – into a parallel universe full of automobiles that you would not expect to see from Porsche and which you would hardly have dared to dream of. We also sometimes had to pinch ourselves to be sure we weren't dreaming. For example when Michael Mauer lifted the covers for us on a modern, road-ready Porsche 911 Safari. Or when the amazingly small prototype of a modern Porsche 904 emerged from storage. Or when we first set eyes on a dramatic, four-door Supersport study, evidence of the incredible story of the development of the Porsche Taycan. That evening, none of us would have been surprised if the design chief had asked us in a friendly but firm tone of voice to stare into a small device that would immediately wipe our memory of everything we had seen.

Why were these cars never built? For Michael Mauer this isn't an important question. Not every good idea has to go into production in order to advance the brand. For him and his team, their experimental work is first and foremost about creating spaces for opportunity and establishing a relationship with the future. Some ideas never get beyond sketches on paper or in virtual space.

其余的想法，有的继续推进，有的被制成了能够直观感受体量与比例的3D模型。有的甚至被制成了最终的原型车并驶上附近的测试道路。所有的这些都代表着一个构想、一种崭新的思考。它们作为灵感为未来提供方向、改变视角，作为可视化辅助工具指导保时捷各个领域员工的决策过程——无论是有意识的还是无意识的。这便是今天的设计师去塑造未来世界的方式，哪怕只是一个想法、一根线条或是一块曲面，都有可能最终变为现实。毛迈恪的设计哲学在整个过程中体现得淋漓尽致——必须在未来发生之前想象出它的样子。

这种独特的哲学似乎可以在魏斯阿赫——这个孕育所有保时捷的地方——被清楚地感知到。设计、发动机研发、车身架构、测试、制造与赛车部门配合无间，精准如同钟表，解决棘手难题的专家与你近在咫尺。开发新产品、新原型车并从用户的角度进行尝试，这种亲密的跨学科团队合作自20世纪70年代以来便一直是魏斯阿赫的常规操作。

无论你是与曾经参与过风冷时期911车型设计的"老手"对话，还是与刚毕业的大学生交谈，都能感受到这个设计工作室中新颖且开放的思维方式。这是一个让人不忍离去的地方——自2004年开始这里便是毛迈恪的主场，在保时捷73年的历史中他也仅仅是自费迪南德·亚历山大·保时捷之后的第三任首席设

Others are taken further and produced as a three-dimensional scale model on which volumes and proportions can be trialed. Some were even built as prototypes and put through their paces on the nearby test track. All of them symbolize an idea, a new concept. They are intended as inspiration, providing orientation, changing perspectives and serving employees in all areas of the company as a visualization aid for decision-making processes – whether conscious or unconscious. This is how the ideas of today's designers shape the world of tomorrow. Even if it is sometimes just an idea, a line or a curve that ultimately becomes reality. Michael Mauer's central philosophy is reflected in this process: you've got to think the future before it can happen.

Maybe its the special Weissach vibe, this energy that can be felt everywhere at the epicenter of the Porsche brand, that makes such a visionary culture possible in the first place. Design, engine development, body construction, testing, production, racing: The individual areas worked together like clockwork. A specialist for every imaginable question is usually only a few minutes' walk away. Design sprints, in which interdisciplinary teams develop new ideas with the help of prototypes and try them out from the user's perspective, have been common practice at Weissach since the 1970s.

It doesn't matter whether you're talking to an "old hand" who can remember working on the air-cooled 911, or a young university graduate, the mindset in the design studio is fresh and open to change. It is a place that people can be reluctant to leave: this has been Michael Mauer's home turf since 2004. He is only the brand's third design boss since F.A. Porsche, who created the Porsche 911 together with his team.

计师，后者与他的团队共同创造出了911这款划时代的车型。

对魏斯阿赫设计工作室的一瞥还可以让我们感受到创新和设计的专业性对保时捷来说究竟有多重要。设计师在公司有着至高无上的地位。毛迈恪与他的设计团队不仅仅是将新产品根据生产中既定选项将其包装得更加光鲜亮丽的造型师，而是从宏观角度出发，将自己视为产品的开发者：作为品牌的智囊团用他们的视野与洞见为暗淡而遥远的未来带来一丝曙光，引领保时捷走向未知世界。

通常，在一个组织严密的汽车制造公司，很少有CEO能够为设计负责人提供这样的创作自由。毕竟，不是每一个来自未来的天马行空的想法都能自动走向为既定目标群体定制的全新量产模式。即便如此，自2015年始掌管保时捷的全球执行董事会主席奥博穆以及他的前任穆勒都选择充分信任毛迈恪和他的团队。他们为新思路创造空间，绕开熟悉的道路，在这个技术和社会瞬息万变的时代中不断创新，"重新发明轮子"。

先进性、革命性设计以及最重要的非凡创意在保时捷的传奇中占据了可观的篇幅，而且成为保时捷的品牌哲学的核心元素。由此，我们不仅能在今时与往日的保时捷产品中看到汽车行业的先锋设计，更能看到其为自己设计的令人兴奋的未来。

A glimpse behind the scenes at the studios in Weissach also shows how important innovation and design expertise are to the Porsche brand. The role of the designers remains paramount within the company. Michael Mauer and his team are much more than just stylists who package each new model attractively according to the predefined options available in production. Instead, they see themselves as product developers who understand their task in holistic terms: brand masterminds whose visions help to shed a little light on the dim and distant future. They aim to help navigate the company's path in a new, unknown world.

It is by no means standard practice for the CEO of a tightly organized automotive company to give his head of design such creative freedom. After all, not every memory of the future, every vision brought back from the world of the day after tomorrow will automatically lead to a new production model tailored to established target groups. Nonetheless, Dr. Oliver Blume, who has been at the helm of Porsche since 2015, and his predecessor Matthias Müller have placed their trust in Michael Mauer and his team. They have created the space to develop new ideas, taking a detour away from familiar paths and constantly reinventing the wheel in times of rapid technological and social change.

Progressiveness, innovative design and, above all, great, unconventional ideas are not just part of Porsche's legacy, but still form central elements in the company's philosophy. Thus, both yesterday and today, Porsche embodies the avantgarde of automotive design – and looks with optimism towards an exciting future that it has designed for itself.

设计过程
The Design Process

一瞥保时捷魏斯阿赫创意工作室的幕后

A Glimpse behind the Scenes at the Ideas Workshop at Porsche in Weissach

上午 8 点半，魏斯阿赫。镇子的广场上坐落着教堂和肉店，连绵起伏的山丘和金色的麦田环绕四围，若不是在街角不时遇到的伪装的原型车，你一定会以为这是一个普通的德国南部小镇。这一派田园牧歌的风光距离保时捷在祖文豪森的总部仅有 25 公里，自 1971 年起，这里便是保时捷研发中心所在地。魏斯阿赫是所有新系列车型诞生的地方——从草图、比例模型到全新发动机、底盘和原型车，后续完成台架测试、风洞测试和道路测试等，以及进入公司自己的测试赛道。各个部门距离很近，交流很多。甚至于保时捷品牌的运动基因也明显地反映在地理位置上——保时捷赛车运动中心位于邻近的弗拉特，距此仅有数百米之遥。风向合适的时候，赛车引擎的轰鸣声会成为设计师、建模师和工程师们的工作伴奏。

"施瓦本人的严肃天性与绝对前卫并存。"毛迈恪如是说。他在 2004 年以首席设计师的身份加入保时捷，很显然他在魏斯阿赫倾注了很多情感。在这里，他与团队设计出了保时捷 Panamera 与 Macan，对 Cayenne 进行了更新换代，创造了里程碑般的 918 Spyder，更对 911 进行了 991、992 两次升级换代。他为这个品牌带来了人们所熟知的家族化设计，这里诞生的很多作品在全球拿下的知名奖项不胜枚举，而毛迈恪也被当作是这个时代最具影响力的设计师之一。然而，当评审和记者问他有关 911 的传承或是最新车型的造型的问题时，他的思考往往着眼于别处，比如说，未来。

这是因为与其他厂商相比，保时捷在设计领域拥有一群专注于描绘未来的人。他们的工作便是尽可能自由地去畅想和探索未来的一切可能性。我们凭借这次特殊的机会得以在这个自行设计的明日世界拜访毛迈恪，查看那些保存在机密设计档案里的概念研究，并在设计工作室神圣的大厅里与毛迈恪聊了聊远见卓识的力量、创新的勇气、未来汽车的样貌，当然还有魏斯阿赫——这个被称为"汽车工业硅谷"的地方。

"保时捷慎重地在研发与制造基地边上搭建了这唯一的设计中心，"毛迈恪解释道，"魏斯阿赫是我们的行动中枢。相比于在北美和亚洲分别成立设计中心，我们将世界各地的设计师聚集到林地环绕的魏斯阿赫，共同创造最新款的运动型车与汽车行业的未来。毕竟硅谷这个名字只有保持原先的地理含义才是真正的不忘初心。"毛迈恪在 20 世纪 90 年代于东京经营过一家设计工

It's 8:30 am in Weissach. This could be any completely normal southern German small town, with a church and butcher shop on the village square, surrounded by rolling hills and golden wheat fields – if it weren't for the Porsche prototypes taped over with camouflage foil that visitors encounter on the road. This idyllic rural setting, just 25 kilometers from the main plant in Zuffenhausen, is where Porsche has had its Development Center since 1971. Weissach is where all new series models are created – from the first drawing and scale models to the development of new engines, chasses and near-series prototypes, which are then tested on the test benches and in the wind tunnels, as well as on the company's own test track. The distances between the various departments are short and exchanges are intense. Even the affinity with racing is evident in geographical terms at Porsche: The Porsche Motorsport Center in the neighboring town of Flacht, where the brand's racing cars are built, is just a few hundred meters away. When the wind is right, the roar of the racing engines rings in the ears of the designers, model builders and engineers as a soundtrack to their work.

"The non-nonsense nature that characterizes the people of Swabia exists side-by-side with the absolute avant-garde," says Michael Mauer. He joined Porsche as Head of Design in 2004 and obviously feels right at home in Weissach. This is where he and his team designed the Porsche Panamera and the Macan, further developing the Cayenne, setting a sporting milestone with the 918 Spyder and reinventing the 911 twice with the 991 und 992 generations. The product ID, the face of the Porsche brand as we know it, is his work. The designs from the Porsche Design Studio are repeatedly awarded the most important international prizes and Michael Mauer is regarded as one of the most influential designers of our time. However, while jurors and journalists ask him about the evolution of the 911 or the silhouettes of the latest production models, his thoughts are usually elsewhere. For example in the future.

That's because, in contrast to many other brands, Porsche relies on special teams for ideas and visions within the design area, whose task it is to experiment as freely as possible and to explore the future of mobility on journeys of the mind. We have been granted the unique opportunity to visit Michael Mauer in this self-designed world of tomorrow, to see some of the concept studies from the secret design archive and to talk to him in the hallowed halls of the Design Studio about the power of visionary thinking, the courage to innovate and the car of tomorrow and, of course, about Weissach – the Silicon Valley of the automotive industry.

"Porsche deliberately only operates a single design studio – in close proximity to Development and Production," explains Michael Mauer. "Weissach is the epicenter for all our activities. Instead of opening advanced design studios in the distant cities of North America and Asia, we bring our designers from all over the world to the heartland of the Porsche brand in the meadows and forests around Weissach to create the latest production sports cars and automotive visions. After all, Silicon

"施瓦本人的严肃天性与绝对前卫并存"

"The non-nonsense nature that characterizes the people of Swabia exists side-by-side with the absolute avant-garde."

作室，这段经历让他深知主场优势的重要性。所以他会将全世界最好的 120 位设计师、内／外饰专家、涂装与材料专家、模型师和概念工程师聚集于魏斯阿赫设计中心——一个采光极好、视野开阔、空间通透并被雾面玻璃包围的空间内。所有的设计师都以专注、自信的方式工作，彼此的交流也充满友善与尊重。伴随着窗外发动机粗哑的吼声，一款全新的产品正在秘密酝酿之中。

"在魏斯阿赫你能够清晰地感受到，设计师与保时捷这个品牌乃至构成它的一切都有着密切的联系。设计师在描绘每一张草图时，就已经看到了原型车在测试赛道上飞驰的样子，"毛迈恪一边解释，一边带着我们走过一排停放在走廊上的还盖着布的等比例模型。这些模型好像好莱坞摄影棚中等待出镜的演员。"同时，在这里工作的每一位设计师都有着极高的自由度，以便在一个毫无限制的环境中肆意表达，能够在这样的环境里相互影响还是很重要的。"每个设计师的工作内容也会有很大的跨度，你可能会在上午为一辆 Macan 的衍生车型贡献创意，下午就要去尝试刻画一款为 2050 年准备的产品。在这里，进化与变革是永恒的主题。"这样的工作模式能够使设计师保持警觉，维持创造力，同时也确保项目之间的交流，更重要的是可以将那些前瞻性的设计更好地落实到量产车的设计中。"

显然，魏斯阿赫几乎没有能让人分心的事情。在著名的夏日派对期间，设计团队会自发地打造一辆"艺术车"，你会在研发中心的后院感受到一点加州科切拉音乐节的气息；当你在设计过程中苦苦寻找灵感，并迫切想仔细看看保时捷917的进气口时，可以直接驱车前往祖文豪森的保时捷博物馆；此外，在食堂吃午饭时，你总有机会与发动机开发、车身制造和赛车部门的专家进行交流。因此，保时捷构想和开发愿景通常都稳固地基于现实。因为无论这些点子看起来多么疯狂，通常都会在风格上参考该

Valley has always stayed true to its original location." Mauer ran a design studio in Tokyo in the 1990s and knows all about home advantage. That's why he has created a studio that is one of the premier addresses for all automotive designers. More than 120 designers, experts in interiors, exteriors, paints and materials, model makers, modelers and concept engineers are employed here. The spaces are airy and bright, with plenty of diffuse daylight cast through tall windows of frosted glass. The designers work in a concentrated, self-assured manner on amazingly realistic clay models. Interactions with one another and with the boss are friendly and respectful. Outside, an engine starts with a hoarse bark. Knowing looks, insider nods – a new model name does the rounds, still a top secret.

"The link between the designer and the Porsche brand – and really everything that defines it – is very strong in Weissach. In every sketch that he is working on, the designer can already visualize how the prototype will look doing its laps on the test site," explains Michael Mauer, leading us past a series of covered scale models that sit in the studio corridors like actors in a Hollywood film waiting for their cue. "At the same time, the designers are allowed maximum freedom here and can express their creativity without restrictions. This interplay is a very special feature. "The range of models the designers work on is also considerable. In the morning you could be working on a derivative model of the Porsche Macan and in the afternoon you find yourself developing a vision for the year 2050. There is a constant switch between evolution and revolution. "This balancing act keeps the designers on their creative toes, as well as ensuring maximum give-and-take between projects. In this way, a visionary design can actually influence the work on series products in a constant creative cycle."

Obviously, there are few distractions in Weissach. Only during the famous summer festivals, where an "art car" can be spontaneously produced, will you find a little Californian Coachella Festival spirit blowing through the backyards of the Development Center. But if you are struggling for inspiration in the design process and urgently want to take a closer look at the air inlets of the Porsche 917, you can take a quick drive across to the in-house museum in Zuffenhausen. In addition, there's always a chance to catch up with the specialists from engine development, body construction and the racing department at

工作室的夏日派对，2018年7月
Studio summer party 07/2018

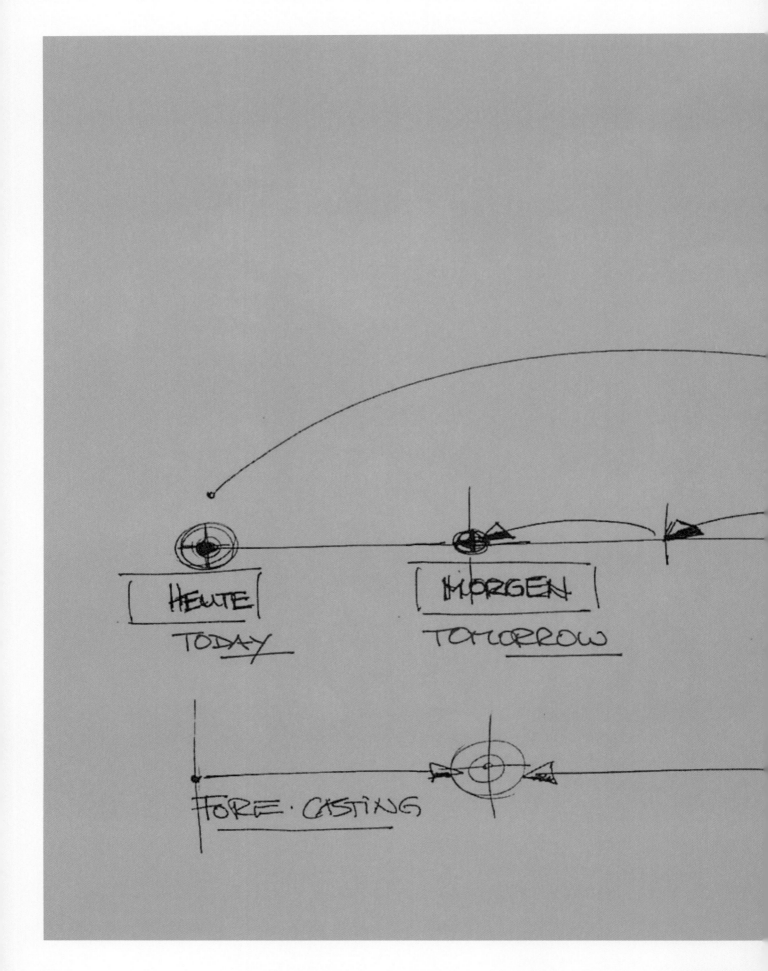

HEUTE
TODAY

MORGEN
TOMORROW

FORE·CASTING

见所未见

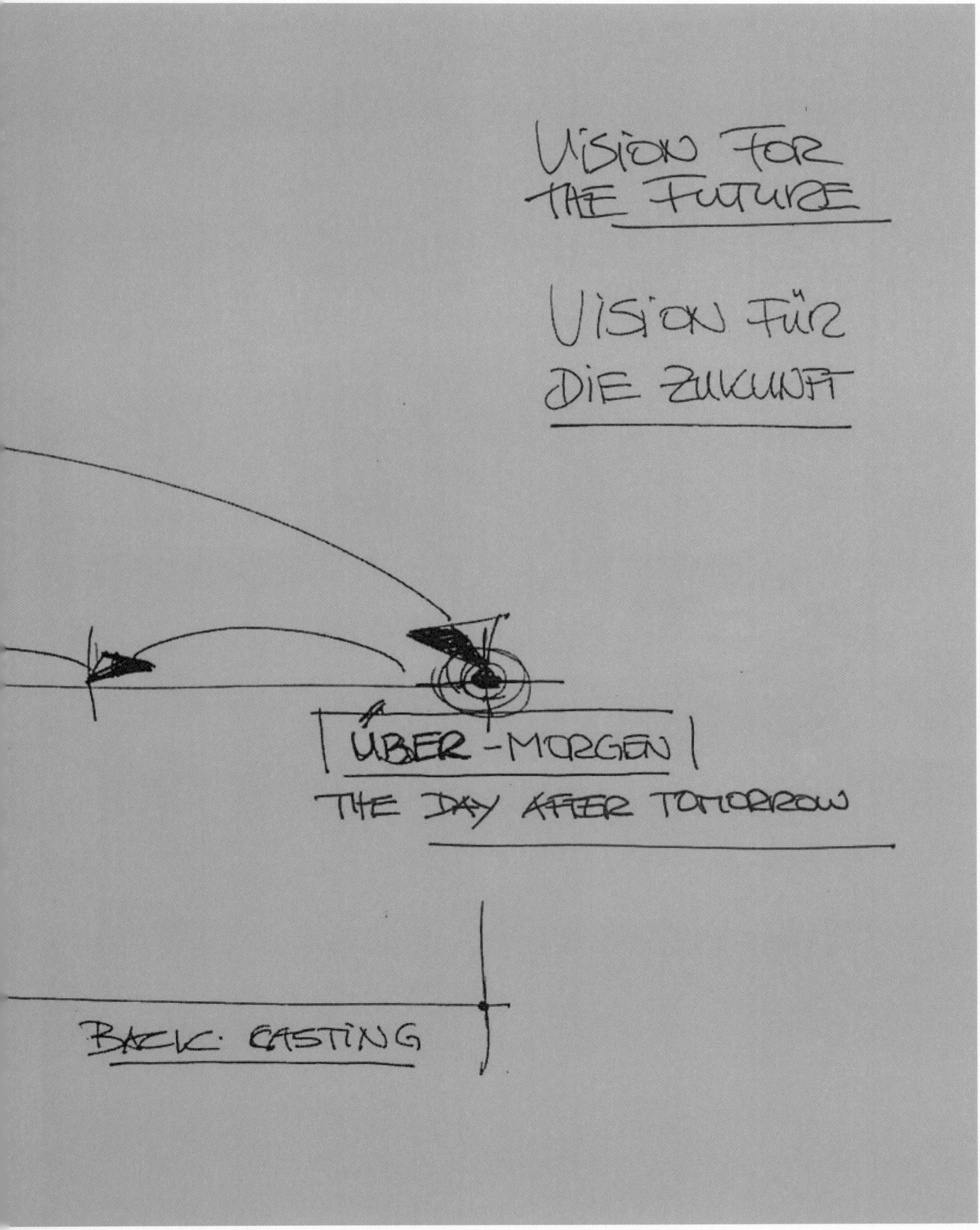

VISION FOR
THE FUTURE

VISION FÜR
DIE ZUKUNFT

| ÜBER - MORGEN |
THE DAY AFTER TOMORROW

BACK. CASTING

保时捷的未来设计

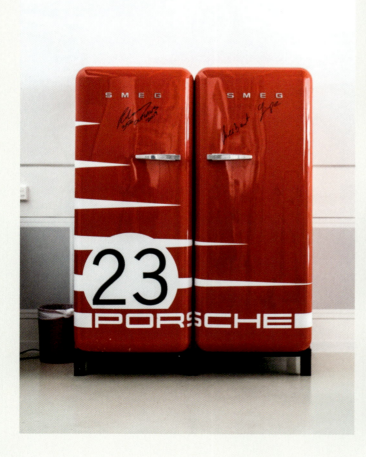

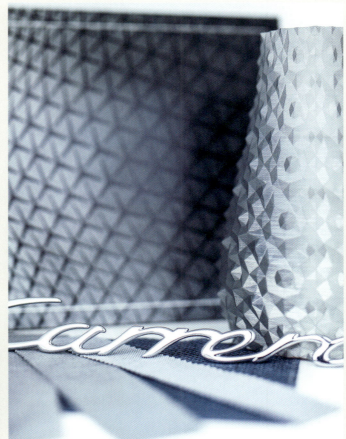

品牌的丰富历史或与当前赛车的技术相连接。这些联系甚至为最具实验性的概念研究提供了独特的风格和特征，并与品牌密切相关，同时也是不可互换的。

回到未来

我向这位资深设计师提出了一个基本问题：为什么愿景对保时捷如此重要？"品牌有两种发展路径，"毛迈恪解释道，"要么基于现有状态改进产品，这将会是一个循序渐进、按部就班的过程。但是这种方法很难真正创新。要么，你可以自由发挥自己的创造力。这便需要你的思绪能够先跳到后天，然后再回到真正需要去到的明天。"在未来的15年、20年甚至30年里你会设计什么样的产品？这种更宏观的视角为进一步推论提供了起点：设计师通过时间倒退，看看使用当前技术可以在5年或10年内实现愿景的哪些初步阶段。设计者将这种基于倒退演绎的方法称为预测和回溯。"我的理论是，这能让你变得更具创新性和现代感。"

我们来看看保时捷 Vision Turismo 吧。这辆诞生于设计工作室的汽车，其最初身份是后置发动机四门超级跑车的研究实验。最终，它成了品牌首款纯电动量产车的原型。"如果仅以量产纯电动车作为最初的设计目标，那么 Taycan 最终的成品将不会拥有现在的模样。假如我们不具备这样的视野，保时捷的设计语言便无法发展到如今的高度。"有时，一些设计项目会向意料之外的方向发展，或者被一些原因间接引导至不同的维度。甚至在有些时候，首席设计师都会困惑一个绝妙的点子该何去何从。不过往往在几个月甚至几年之后，这个点子可能会重新浮出水面成为另一个问题的答案，更有甚者，会成为一项全新科技的应用案例。

站在消费者或者局外人的角度看，每一辆驶下生产线的保时捷都宛如一曲完美、连贯的乐章。和一部成功的电影、一本获奖的书籍、一张畅销的专辑一样，我们将其视为不可替代的杰作。我们看不见的研发过程被隐匿在创意的黑匣子中。即便是保时捷911，它的诞生过程也不是那么一气呵成。这款代表性车型的研发历史更像是曲折的试错过程，有太多灵感被尝试，又最终被放弃。你只需去保时捷博物馆寻找一辆名为754 T7的金属绿色的原型车，由 F.A. 保时捷带领团队在1960年设计，这是保时捷911的先驱作品。那时你才会真正理解，在创作汽车的杰作之前，往往要尽心竭力地寻找恰当的比例、理想的线条和完

lunch in the canteen. Thus, the visions conceived and developed at Porsche usually have one wheel firmly based in reality. Because, no matter how crazy they might seem, there is often a stylistic reference to the rich history of the brand or a technological link to current racing. These connections give even the most experimental concept studies a distinctive style and character and great relevance for the brand. They are anything but interchangeable.

Back to Tomorrow

A fundamental question for the senior designer: why are visions so important to Porsche? "There are two ways in which a brand can develop," explains Michael Mauer. "Either you improve your products based on the present, that is in an evolutionary, step-by-step process. However, it is difficult to be really innovative in this approach. Alternatively, you can allow your creativity free rein. The idea is to let your mind skip for ward to the day after tomorrow and from there back to tomorrow." What products might you find yourself building in 15, 20 or 30 years? This grand vision provides the starting point for further deductions: The designers move backwards through time and look at which preliminary stages of a vision could be achieved in five or ten years' time using the technology currently available. The designers refer to this as forecasting and backcasting. "My theory is that this enables you to be much more innovative and modern."

We take a sideways glance at the Porsche Vision Turismo. The shiny silver prototype was initially developed in the Design Studio as an experimental study for a super sports car with four doors and a rear engine. In the end, however, it served as a blueprint for the brand's first fully electric production model. "A Porsche Taycan would now look quite different if it had started off as a project for a production electric car. The Porsche design language would not have developed in this way if we did not have such scope." Sometimes a project takes an unexpected direction or leads by indirections to a point you would never have expected at the start of the conceptual work. Sometimes even the Head of Design is faced with a fascinating idea that he doesn't know exactly what to with. Then months or even years later, this idea bubbles up to the surface from the depths of the subconscious as the solution to a completely different problem. Or even as an example of how a completely new technology could be used.

As customers and external observers, we tend to see each new production car as a perfect, coherent ensemble. This is the same way we see a successful film, an award-winning book, or a hit album as a discrete masterpiece with no alternatives. The development work within the black box of creativity usually remains hidden from us. But not even the Porsche 911 was born full-fledged as an ingenious design on a blank sheet of paper. The development history of the brand icon can be seen rather as a complex process of trial-and error, in which more ideas were tried and cast aside than pursued. You only have to look at the Porsche Museum's metallic green Porsche 754 T7 designed in 1960 by F.A. Porsche and his team as a precursor of the first Porsche 911. That's when you really begin to understand that the creation of an automotive

美的曲面。

"我们的研发目标并不是将每一辆车都开上路，我们更加关注的是探索更多可能性以及与未来建立某种联系，"谈及设计过程，毛迈恪说道，"对一个虚拟的概念进行探索是十分艰巨的，这项工作改变了我，也改变了我思考的方式。毕竟，当我花了很多时间在脑海里构想未来时，这也会影响我看待当下的角度。"之后呢？"勾勒一个未来的概念用不了很久，难的是将这个概念一步步变为能够触碰的实体，并让它与当下的世界建立连接。"那么这些关于将来的畅想对量产车有何影响？如何将虚构的科幻变成现实？"每一个系列项目都会按照特定的节奏进行，通常需要在数月之内完成，如果你能在此过程中挖掘利用这些想法和概念研究，那么成果自然而然地会颇具革新性。这就是如何让设计团队和品牌设计语言保持新鲜感的方法，当然这也是你源源不断的灵感源泉。"如果没有关于保时捷在未来10年、15年或20年的畅想，那么品牌与产品策略的进一步发展也是不可想象的。

尽管以上一切听起来都足够合理，但这肯定不是一个显而易见的答案，毕竟，你确实无法基于保时捷大量研究项目所展现出的洞见去判断它们是否以及如何影响了当下的量产车。所以，当市场调研可以精确地展现当今客户想要什么时，为什么要花如此多的时间考虑遥远的未来呢？"开发一款全新的量产车是一个漫长的过程。如果缺乏远见，五年后上市的汽车将重复今天的设计语言，"毛迈恪解释道，"那样的话我们便无法通过革新来引领新的潮流，只能原地踏步。"

毕竟，我们生活在一个瞬息万变的时代，社会与科技飞速变化。对于保时捷这样成功的汽车制造商来说，以新的理念预测出行的发展趋势至关重要。你必须改变看待事物的方式进而推出引领潮流的新产品，而不是随波逐流。这需要冒险的胆识与魄力和创业的勇气，最重要的是信任那些代表品牌去探索未来更多可能性的有远见的人。

毛迈恪成功说服了他最重要的支持者——CEO奥博穆博士，他允许设计部门自由地投资给研究，以此来产出更多出色的创意与创新作为回报，而这正是打造未来产品的基础。"我一直想用大部分预算支持一些特别疯狂的想法。我甚至想找一些令人难以置信的汽车，看它们能否最终变成一辆保时捷。"毛迈恪珍视

masterpiece is often preceded by a wearisome search for the right proportions, the ideal line and the perfect overall package.

"The point of the visions we develop is not to get every car onto the road. We are far more concerned with creating areas of opportunity and establishing a relationship with the future," says Michael Mauer with regard to the design process. "This is really tough conceptual work that changes both myself and the way I think. After all, once I have spent some time in the future in my mind, this also changes my view of the present." What then? "It doesn't take long to sketch out a vision of the future. The challenge, however, is to make the idea a reality step-by-step and to establish the link with today's world." So how do the visions of the future influence production cars? How does science fiction become hard reality? "All series projects have a very clear rhythm and have to be completed within a certain number of months. If you can tap into the ideas and concept studies in these processes, the series products automatically become more innovative. This is how to keep the design language of your products and the team working on them fresh, as well as laying the foundation of ideas that you can use." The further development of the brand and portfolio strategy would also be inconceivable without specific ideas about where Porsche might be in 10, 15 or 20 years.

Although this all sounds reasonable enough, it is anything but self-evident – after all, with most of the visions from Porsche's extensive research program, it is impossible to tell whether and how they will influence series production. So why spend so much time thinking about the distant future when market analyses can tell you exactly what customers are looking for right now? "Developing a new production model is a long drawn out process. If it weren't for visions, the cars that reach the market in five years' time would repeat the same design language as today's," explains Michael Mauer. "Instead of setting new trends through innovations, we'd be treading water."

After all, the technological and social changes that characterize the times we live in happen fast. For a successful automobile manufacturer like Porsche it is essential to anticipate the development of mobility with new ideas. You have to change the way you look at things and launch new products that set trends instead of following them. This requires a willingness to take risks, entrepreneurial courage – and above all trust in the visionaries who experiment and explore the future on behalf of the brand.

Michael Mauer has managed to convince his most important backer, CEO Dr. Oliver Blume to allow the design sector the freedom to invest in research – and to be rewarded with ideas and innovations in return. These are the foundations of the products of the future. "I always wanted to use a substantial part of the budget to produce some particularly crazy ideas. I was looking for cars that might make you shake your head at first and wonder whether they could be a Porsche at all." Michael Mauer values the freedom to question the traditions and conventions of the brand in a playful way. This ignites internal discussions and redefines the central

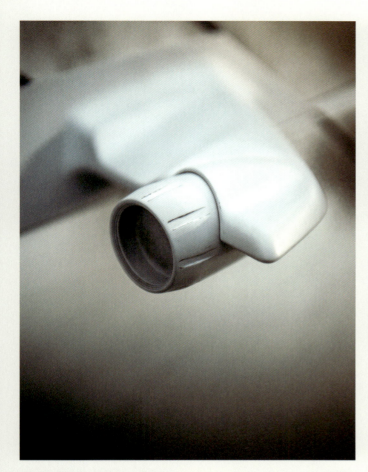

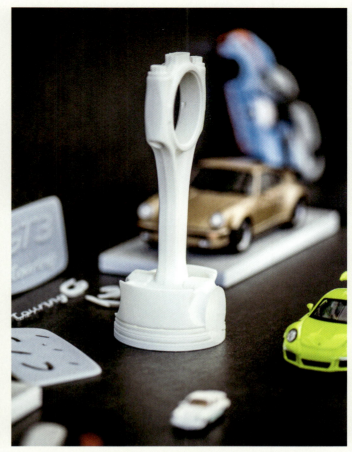

保时捷的未来设计

能以有趣的方式质疑品牌传统和惯例的自由，因为这样可以激发内部的充分讨论，并一次次地重新定义保时捷的核心价值观。

史蒂夫·乔布斯和乔纳森·艾夫的无间合作指出了加州硅谷技术领域成功的关键，这种有着自由思想的企业家与前卫设计师结合的方式也让汽车行业看到了复兴的机会。"当 CEO 有信心让团队拥有如此的创作自由时，他与首席设计师之间的关系也会向一个更加积极的方向发展。"毛迈恪承认，"为了实现这一点，CEO 也必须是一个有远见的人。"

从第一张草图到可驾驶的原型车

在我们的这次造访中所见的不少设想是以草图或比例模型的形式呈现的，其余一些车则非常接近量产状态，似乎已经准备好上路了。毛迈恪为他和团队的实验性项目做了区分，其中一部分是以保时捷911、Macan 或 718 Cayman 等成功车型为基础，探索其潜力，不断衍生、变化而来。

比如说以各式经典车型为基础的自带越野属性的 Safari（穿越非洲拉力赛）版本或者讲究纯粹主义的 Bergspyder（爬山赛车）版本。这些引人注目的车可以作为限量版特别系列发行，或是可以完全融入在售产品线的车身变种。通常，这些车型的规格清单非常明确：基于量产车框架，这些特殊车型在未来五年内有面世的可能。

在首席设计师与他的团队心中，向保时捷904或550 Spyder 致敬的轻量化、纯粹且灵活的跑车一直占有一席之地。毛迈恪坚信，一辆出众的紧凑型轻量化跑车在今天依旧会让保时捷的拥趸们趋之若鹜。此外，有朝一日可能会取代保时捷918 Spyder 的新型超级跑车研究项目也格外引人瞩目：这辆车的许多设计灵感来源于在勒芒夺冠的LMP1组别原型赛车以及首次在电动方程式上亮相的保时捷赛车。这些优秀的汽车设计作为竞速类的旗舰项目，相比目前较为成功但更加拘谨的保时捷公路跑车和 SUV 来说，是一种激进的平衡。

这个设计中心还诞生了一些非常疯狂的想法，用毛迈恪的话来说，设计师们"将他们手中的鹅卵石扔进了一口名为未来的深井里"。在这里，设计师们已经将当下抛在了脑后，转而尝试在保时捷品牌中尚不存在的模子和想法。这些富有远见的汽车设计方案多用于策略的讨论、将抽象的想法具象化以及突破传统

values of Porsche over and over again.

The combination of a free-thinking entrepreneur and avant-garde designer that Steve Jobs and Jony Ive established as the key to success in the tech scene in California's Silicon Valley also seems to offer a significant opportunity for the renewal of the automotive industry. "It paints a positive picture of the CEO and his relationship with his Head of Design when he has the confidence to allow the team such creative freedom," Michael Mauer admits. "In order for this to happen, the CEO also has to be a visionary too."

From the First Drawing to the Drivable Prototype

Some of the visions that we see on our tour are sketches or scale models. Other cars, on the other hand, are surprisingly close to series production and just seem to be waiting to hit the road. Michael Mauer differentiates between various categories of projects on which he and his team work. On the one hand there are the derivatives of successful series models such as the Porsche 911, the Macan or the 718 Cayman, the potential of which is under constant exploration through variations.

This could be an off-road Safari version or a purist Bergspyder based on a historical model. Fascinating cars that can be issued as limited edition special series – or body variants that would simply fit well into the brand portfolio. The specification sheets for these models are usually very specific: It must be possible to implement the variations in the next five years within the framework of series production.

An automotive genre that is particularly close to the heart of the Head of Design and his team is the small, purist and agile sports car with echoes of lightweight construction icons such as the Porsche 904 or 550 Spyder. Michael Mauer is convinced that a compact agile race car would still inspire the sporty brand community today. The studies for a new hypersports car that could one day succeed the Porsche 918 Spyder are particularly dramatic: Many designs are inspired by the victories of the LMP1 racing cars in Le Mans and the brand's first outings in Formula E. As racing flagship projects, these impressive automotive visions act as a radical counterweight to the more restrained touring sports cars and SUVs that are garnering Porsche so much success at present.

And then there are the crazy ideas in which the designers – in Michael Mauer's word – "cast their pebbles into the waters of the very far future." Here the designers leave the present behind to experiment with shapes and ideas that as yet do not exist at Porsche. These visionary cars are used to discuss strategies, visualize abstract ideas and push the boundaries of tradition and convention. Things can quickly get quite philosophical in internal discussions: What actually is a Porsche? What is it not? What body shapes and spatial concepts are possible? Could there ever be a self-driving Porsche? What does sportiness actually mean? What comes after the automobile as we know it today?

与惯例。在内部讨论中，问题很快会上升到哲学层面：保时捷究竟是什么？什么不能算是保时捷？怎样的身形与空间的概念是可行的？一辆自动驾驶的保时捷可能存在吗？运动性到底意味着什么？我们今天所熟知的汽车以后会是什么样子？

基于这些问题，公司未来的发展方向被持续不断地讨论着。然而，回到现实：未来愿景的设计过程与量产车究竟有何不同？谁来决定一个想法的去留？对此毛迈恪放慢了语速解释道："设计组是开发部门的一部分，新量产车的开发过程高度民主，许多来自不同部门的员工都有发言权。但是，如果你想让不同寻常的想法得以继续，在项目开始时牵扯太多人反而会导致效率低下。这就是为什么我们被获准可以直接从 CEO 那里获得预算的原因。奥博穆和设计副总裁可以最先听到所有新的想法。"

颇具前瞻性的新项目的大多数都来自设计组内部。"你问自己：一辆能乘坐四人甚至六人的保时捷是什么样子？之后你开始自由地勾勒你的设计，最终形成一个草稿。"与量产车不同，创作的自由并不会受到特定技术的限制，例如发动机、变速箱、底盘组件等。整个设计过程由草图开始，继而被生成可视化的3D 模型。如果一个想法得到 CEO 以及研发和销售副总裁的批准，就会制作出比例为1：3的小模型，之后是最终的1：1比例的硬质模型。"虚拟现实是第一步，但那些不同寻常的设计方案需要通过三维模型来理解它们的体量以及精巧的比例。"毛迈恪说。并且如果一个方案的内饰设计特别重要，我们也会专门打造一个带有完整座舱设计的模型。

开发过程接近尾声时，会诞生一辆带有发动机、变速箱和所有技术架构的可驾驶原型车。如新款保时捷911等系列车型，总会有多种设计方案互相角逐。它们已进入了相当高级的设计阶段，并呈现了具体的模型。在他们富有远见的项目中，设计师会专注于一个能够被提炼成核心想法的方案并持续执行下去。

保时捷的大多数设计研究的成果看起来都非常切实可行，这得归结为专业的任务分工。拥有丰富量产车经验的模型制造师与设计师一起工作，工作室工程师需要确保这些概念设计至少在基本技术上是可行的。车身制造师、发动机工程师和声学专家也以他们的专业知识提供支援。"当我们的设计师想要展现他们的成果时，很快就会有接近一个量产项目的一半的人力加入，"毛迈恪笑着说，"设计师需要时刻记住，当一个项目决定量产，

The future direction of the company is under constant discussion based on these questions. But, back to the present: How does the process of designing a vision differ from that of a production car – and who decides whether an idea should be pursued or dropped? Michael Mauer slows his pace to explain: "The Design Group is part of the Development Department and the development of a new production vehicle is a highly democratic process in which a lot of people from different groups have a say. However, if you are also looking to develop unusual and special ideas, it can be counterproductive if too many people are involved at the start. That's why it is agreed that we receive our budget directly from the CEO. Hence Oliver Blume and the Vice President Design are the first to hear all new ideas."

Most ideas for new visionary projects come from within the Design Group itself. "You ask yourself: What could a Porsche for four or even six people look like? Then you begin to sketch out your designs freely. The final result is a draft." Unlike series production, creative freedom is not restricted by defined technical packages, such as engines, transmissions, floorpan assemblies and axles. The design process begins with a sketch, which is visualized in virtual space as a 3D model in the next step. If an idea meets the approval of the CEO and the Vice Presidents Development and Sales, small 1:3 scale models are produced, followed by a final 1:1 scale hard model. "Virtual reality is the first step, but it is precisely the more unusual models that have to be experienced in three dimensions in order to understand how small, big or surprisingly proportioned a car might be," says Michael Mauer. If the interior is of particular importance, we might also build a model with a fully designed cockpit.

At the end of the development process you have a drivable prototype with engine, gearbox and all the technological architecture. With series models such as a new Porsche 911, several designs always compete with each other. They are all taken to quite an advanced stage in the design process and are given concrete shape as models. In their visionary projects, the designers concentrate on a single draft that serves as the protagonist and symbol of the central idea.

Most of the design studies produced at Porsche look incredibly realistic. This is down to the professional division of tasks. Model makers with extensive experience in series production work alongside the designers. Studio engineers ensure that the concepts are technically feasible in fundamental terms at least. Body builders, engine developers and acoustics specialists also support the process with their expertise. "When we designers want to show what we're made of, things can quickly turn into something almost half the size of a series project," says Mauer with a laugh. "You always have to bear in mind that you have to keep your promises when series production is decided. That's why our concept cars for the Porsche 918 and Taycan have always been very close to series-readiness."

This has many advantages in the journey from the drawing board to the streets. But can designers who have internalized

你必须信守承诺。这就是为什么我们为保时捷918 Spyder 和 Taycan 设计的各种概念车一直非常接近量产水平。"

这大大促进了一个想法从手绘板落地到量产出街的过程。但是，已经将这些复杂流程与系统性知识烂熟于胸的设计师们能否在试验项目中摆脱这些"桎梏"，并跨过自身在灵感面前的障碍？"的确，你工作的时间越长，就越会意识到上述这些限制，人是很难摆脱自己熟悉的知识体系的。解决的办法就是用尽可能不同背景的人组成团队，以便经验迥异的人们都可以为项目出力。"保时捷的设计团队实际上拥有经典的人员架构——具有外部、内部和跨学科的职责分配。此外，也有一些团队只做先期开发，前瞻设计以及——简单地说——未来的事。每个团队大约由四到五人组成。

"学生的设计作品也格外天马行空且尚未被现行的规则所束缚，"毛迈恪说，"作为一名成熟老练的设计师，当你看到这些草图时会思索：这些家伙还有很多东西得学。但这种开放的视角正是我们所需要的。这也是为什么在我们的概念设计团队里，那些经验不足但创意十足的设计师占大多数。"在保时捷，刚从大学毕业的年轻设计师可以为品牌的发展贡献自己的想法——而不是无止境地创作最终会被丢进垃圾桶的新车草图。

不同的世界

为了将自己从认知桎梏中解放出来并探索更多奇妙的可能性，毛迈恪很享受与汽车行业之外的设计机构交流思想——比如好莱坞。2019年，保时捷的设计团队与来自卢卡斯影业的特效专家们共同为《星球大战》的奇幻宇宙设计了一款太空载具——三翼 S-91x 珀伽索斯星际战士。事实上，你真的可以在这艘紧凑型宇宙飞船上看到无数让人联想到保时捷设计语言的比例和细节。谁能想到保时捷911经典的车顶线条放在宇宙飞船上竟然如此恰如其分？毛迈恪之所以对这个合作项目津津乐道是因为两个团队工作方式的异同："卢卡斯影业的设计过程和想法的实施方式与我们非常相似。尽管我们也有自己的远见，但汽车设计师在将自己的设想量产化的过程中必须做减法。而《星球大战》团队则可以在实施过程中保持充分的创造力。好莱坞设计师可以自由地决定未来宇宙飞船的驱动源可以只有烟盒一般大小。"但魏斯阿赫所有引擎开发人员的目标却是非常清楚的。

尽管热爱科幻小说也许不是成为优秀产品设计师的必要条件，

all of the processes associated with highly complex and efficient series production break away from this knowledge in experimental projects and free themselves from their own personal barriers to inspiration? "It's quite true that the longer you're in the job, the more aware you become of the restrictions. It is hard to shake off this knowledge. The solution is to put teams together with individuals from as diverse backgrounds as possible, so that people with very different experiences can contribute to a project." The design team at Porsche actually has a classic structure – with exterior, interior and interdisciplinary functions. In addition, however, there are teams that only work on advance development, dealing with visionary design and – to put things simply – the future. There are four to five people from each area.

"Student designs are also often very free and not yet tied down by the rules of what is feasible," says Michael Mauer. "As an experienced designer, you look at these drafts and think: these guys have a lot to learn. But it is precisely this open-minded perspective that we need. That is why the number of designers with little experience but plenty of creativity is particularly high in our concept teams." At Porsche, young designers who have just graduated from university can contribute their ideas to the development of the brand – instead of filling the waste bins with endless variations of new series models.

Different Worlds

In order to free himself from restrictions and to explore the possibilities of the fantastic, Michael Mauer also appreciates the chance to exchange ideas with creative branches outside the automotive industry – for example with Hollywood. Together with the special effects specialists from Lucasfilm, in 2019 the Porsche design team designed a space glider for the Star Wars™ fantasy universe: the Tri-Wing S-91x Pegasus Starfighter. And in fact, you really can see numerous proportions and details in the compact spaceship that are reminiscent of Porsche's design language. Who would have thought that the typical Porsche 911 Flyline would look so good on a starfighter? What fascinated Michael Mauer about the joint project were the similarities and differences in the way the two teams worked: "The design process and the way ideas are implemented at Lucasfilm are very similar to ours. We also have our own visionary ideas. But while an automobile designer has to retrench step-by-step to achieve series readiness, the Star Wars™ team can also remain fully creative in their implementation. The Hollywood designer has the freedom to decide that the drive source for a spaceship will in future only be as small as a cigarette packet." The objective for all engine developers in Weissach is crystal clear.

Although a love of science fiction may not be part of the classic requirement profile for a product designer. But would the technological progress achieved in the 20th century have been possible without visions of flying cars, glass cities on the ocean floor and rotating space stations? Didn't the futuristic worlds created by artists like Syd Mead influence entire

但如果没有飞行汽车、海底玻璃城市和旋转空间站的设想，20世纪取得的技术进步是否有可能实现？像席德·米德这样的艺术家创造的未来世界不是影响了几代设计师吗？

But would the technological progress achieved in the 20th century have been possible without visions of flying cars, glass cities on the ocean floor and rotating space stations? Didn't the futuristic worlds created by artists like Syd Mead influence entire generations of designers?

但如果没有飞行汽车、海底玻璃城市和旋转空间站的设想，20世纪取得的技术进步是否有可能实现？像席德·米德这样的艺术家创造的未来世界不是影响了几代设计师吗？如果《星际迷航》没有在我们的脑海中植入方便的通信和测量设备的想法，iPhone 会如此成功吗？

这样看来，我们的确需要远见、乌托邦概念和更美好的世界的图景，并且依靠它们激发我们的想象力、加速变革、实现创新，并使不可思议的事情变得触手可及。如果没有范例，我们最终会发现所谈论的未来是虚无缥缈的。因此，毛迈恪与他的团队用今日的设计塑造了明日的世界。

"我们的目标并不是实现每一个想法，而是去尝试，跳出思维定式，开辟新的可能性，去感受未来，"毛迈恪在参观开始时说道，"我们的一些设想当前还无法实现。然而，这些设想确实象征着保时捷目前所选择的方向。它们就像指南针，一路为我们提供方向和灵感。"这是魏斯阿赫设计工作室独特的文化理念和实验精神的标志，保时捷现在开放了这座梦工厂，带着我们所有人踏上一段旅程，进入保时捷所打造的运动化出行的未来。

generations of designers? Would the iPhone have been so successful if Star Trek hadn't already planted the idea of a handy communication and measuring device in our heads?

It seems that we need visions, Utopian concepts and images of a better world in order to stimulate our imagination, accelerate change, enable innovations and make the unthinkable thinkable. Without examples, we ultimately find ourselves discussing the future in a vacuum. Thus Michael Mauer and his team shape the world of tomorrow with their designs of today.

"Our goal is not to implement every idea, but rather to give it a try, to think outside the box, to open up new possibilities, to feel the future," said Michael Mauer at the beginning of our tour. "Some of the visions that we develop cannot be implemented at present. However, they do symbolize a direction taken. They can act like a compass, providing orientation and inspiration along the way." It is a further sign of the distinctive culture of ideas and the experimental spirit at the Weissach design studios that Porsche has now opened up its dream factory, taking us all on a journey – into the future of sporty mobility from the Porsche brand.

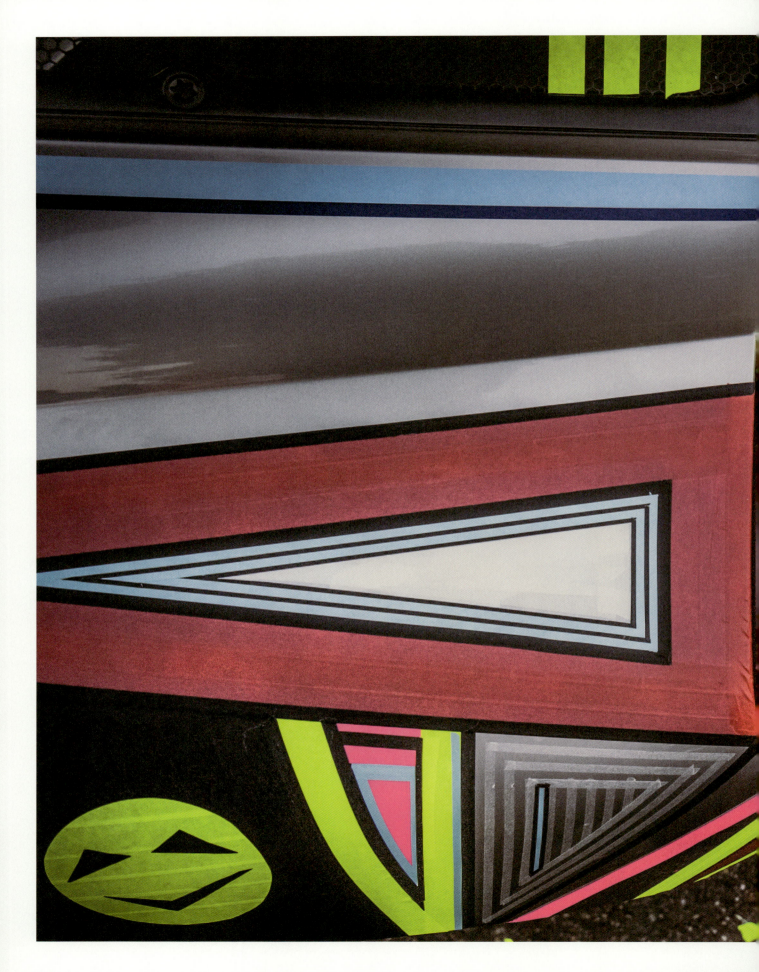

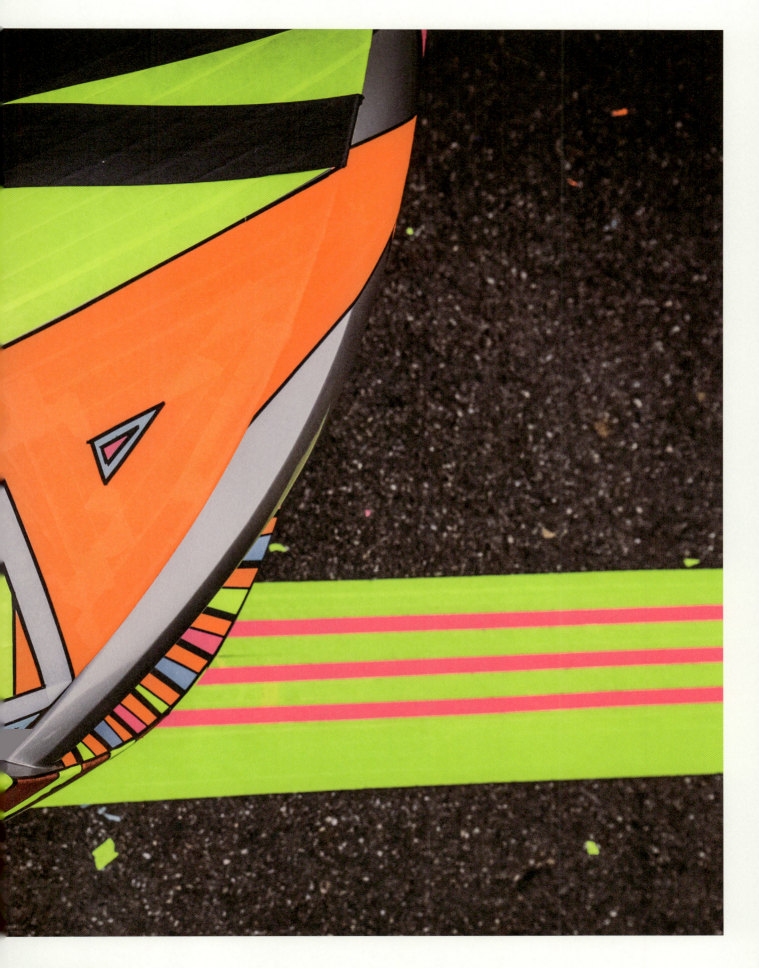

实例探究
Case Studies

意外之喜
Spin-offs and Derivatives

Porsche Boxster Bergspyder
Porsche Le Mans Living Legend
Porsche 911 Vision Safari
Porsche Macan Vision Safari

保时捷不断扩展成功车系的能力已臻化境。仅保时捷911就在过去的50多年间持续出新，比如擅长走街的运动跑车、叱咤赛场的竞速机器，甚至是越野拉力赛车。

所有车系都在保时捷设计中心里经过了一轮又一轮的演化，它们的潜力被挖掘，新的细分市场被锁定，衍生车型的适销性被测试，未来的特别限定系列在这里被创造。一次又一次，品牌的历史成为永不枯竭的灵感源泉。

Porsche has mastered the art of varying a successful automobile like no other brand. It is not just the Porsche 911 that has constantly appeared in new forms for more than 50 years – as a street athlete, an all-conquering race car, or even an off-road rally sports vehicle.

All model series are varied over and over again in the Porsche Design Center. Potential is explored, new niche markets are identified, derivatives are tested for their marketability and tomorrow's limited edition special series are created. Again and again, the brand history serves as an almost inexhaustible source of inspiration.

Porsche Boxster Bergspyder

年份: 2014
Year: 2014

研发状态: 可行驶原型车
Stage of development
Drivable prototype

自20世纪50年代以来，保时捷便凭借着身形小巧的轻量化赛车统治了山路赛车运动。当保时捷910 Bergspyder 在1967年、1968年摘得欧洲爬山锦标赛的桂冠时，保时捷赛车部门的工程师们为费迪南德·皮耶希准备了一辆更为激动人心的作品——保时捷909 Bergspyder。借助其激进的轻量化技术，这辆试图制霸山路的赛车仅有384公斤，这也使其成为保时捷参赛历史上最轻的车辆。尽管这款赛车并没有取得最终胜利，但其极致轻量化的追求还是令人们印象深刻。

由毛迈恪与他的团队设计的保时捷 Boxster Bergspyder 便是向那辆传奇赛车致敬的作品。同时，设计师展示了 Boxster 981系列轻量和强大的中置发动机也非常适合应对阿尔卑斯山曲折的弯道。舍弃了舒适，这辆 Boxster Bergspyder 配备被截短的前挡风玻璃、独特的防倾杆、来自918 Spyder 的仪表盘，后方是一个独特的防滚架，副驾驶座椅也被取消，取而代之的是一个能够放置头盔的架子。这辆车已准备好去挑战最高的山峰。相比于来自 Cayman GT4 的 3.8 升发动机，最大功率 393 马力，车身仅重 1130 公斤，而推重比达到了 2.8 公斤 / 马力。

保时捷 Boxster Bergspyder 首次与公众见面是在2019年的盖斯贝格爬山赛上，现在它与前辈一起在保时捷博物馆展出。

Porsche had dominated alpine motorsport with its small, lightweight racing cars since the late 1950s. While the Porsche 910 Bergspyder won the European hill climb championships in style in 1967 and 1968, the racing engineers had produced an even more dramatic car for Ferdinand Piëch – the Porsche 909 Bergspyder. Thanks to its radical lightweight design, this mountain-conquering vehicle weighed in at only 384 kilos. This makes it the lightest racing car ever deployed by Porsche in motorsport. Even though it was denied the big win, the Porsche 909 Bergspyder is impressive proof of just what can be achieved in terms of weight reduction.

The Porsche Boxster Bergspyder is a tip of the hat from Michael Mauer and his design team to the legendary alpine athlete. At the same time, the designers have shown that the Boxster 981 series, with its low weight and powerful mid-engine, is also ideally suited to negotiating the curves and bends of the Alps. Lacking all comforts, with a capped windshield, a distinctive roll bar, the precision instruments from the Porsche 918, a seat for the driver and a helmet rack instead of the front passenger seat, the Porsche Boxster Bergspyder was ready to hit the highest summits. The weight of 1,130 kilograms contrasted with the 393 hp of the 3.8 liter engine from the Cayman GT4, while the power-to-weight ratio was just 2.8 kilograms per hp.

The Porsche Boxster Bergspyder was unveiled to the public for the first time at the Gaisberg mountain race in 2019. It now forms part of the collection at the Porsche museum – together with its lightweight predecessor and namesake.

1968年，旺图山，罗尔夫·施托梅伦驾驶着保时捷 909 Bergspyder
1968 Mont Ventoux, Rolf Stommelen in the Porsche 909 Bergspyder

见所未见

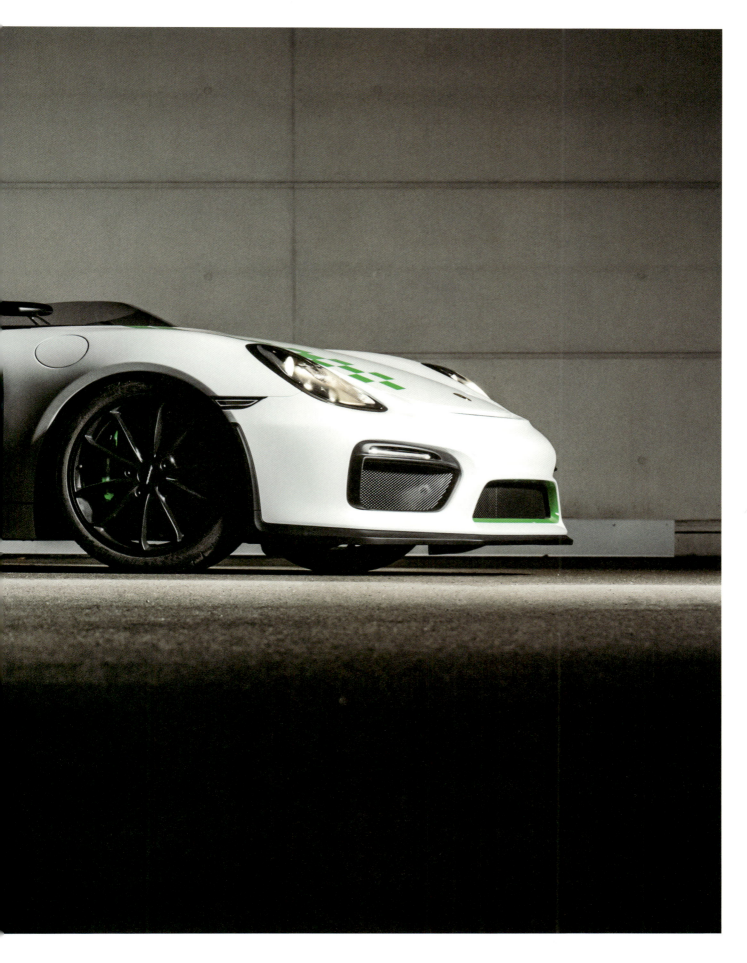

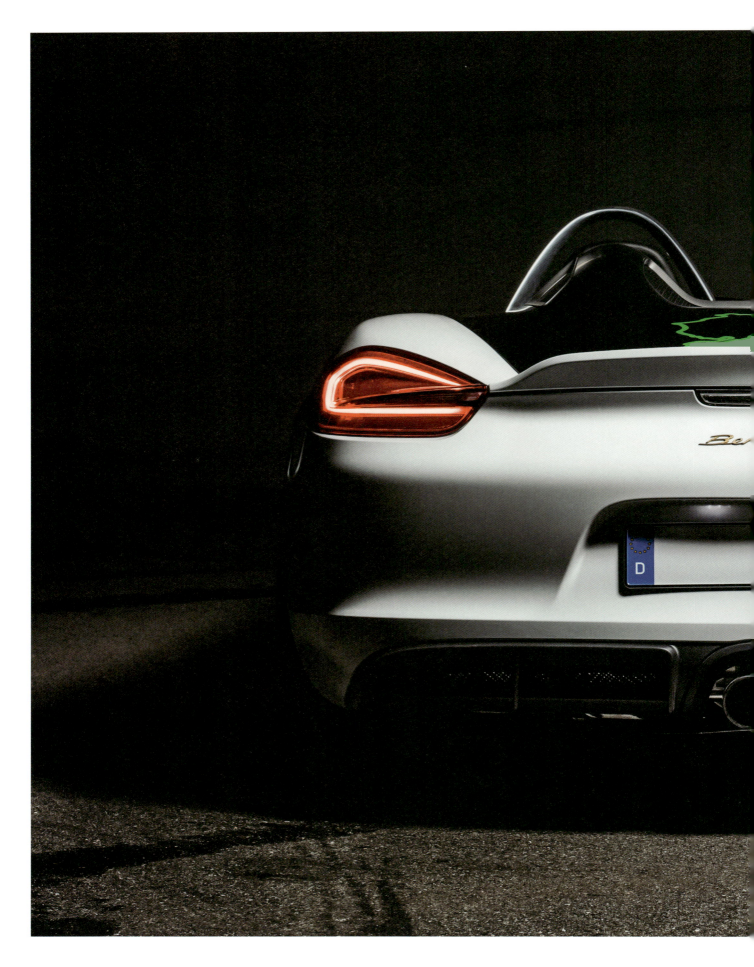

Porsche Le Mans
Living Legend

年份: 2016
Year: 2016

研发状态: 1:1硬质模型
Stage of development
Hard model, scale 1:1

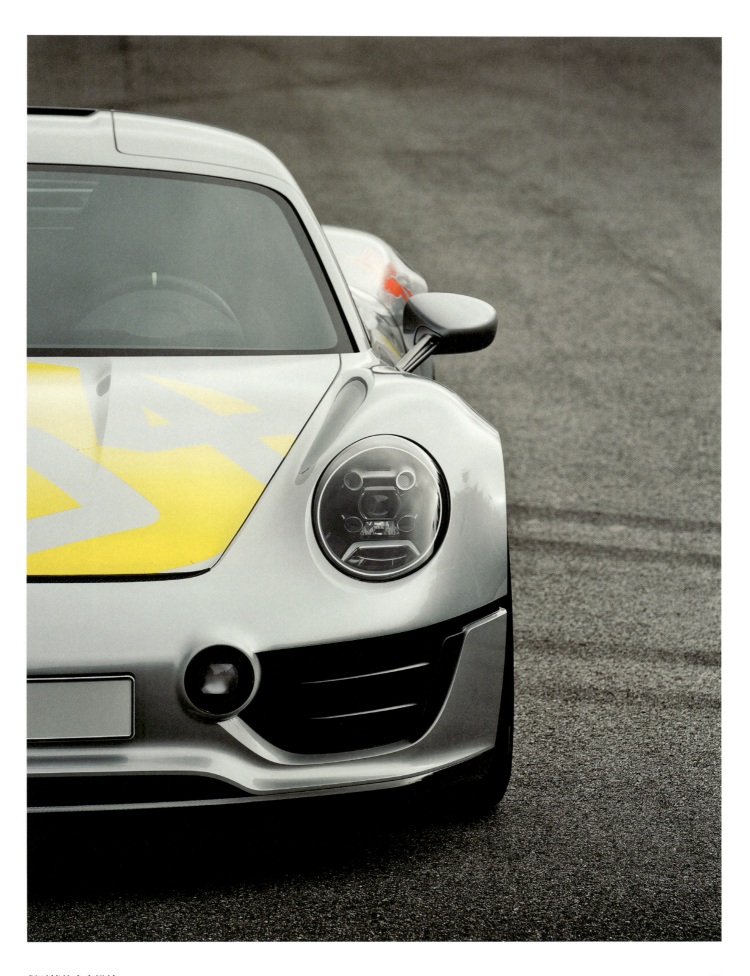

保时捷550总是以"纯粹主义者的敞篷跑车"的形象被人们记住。它作为保时捷首款赛车出现在勒芒时，还有着斯图加特－祖文豪森专为赛道设计的闭合车顶。1953年的勒芒24小时耐力赛上，这辆78马力、中置发动机驱动的550公斤重的跑车首次亮相。驾驶它的则是传奇车手赫尔穆特"Helm"格洛克勒和汉斯·赫尔曼。2016年，这辆开创性的硬顶赛车给魏斯阿赫的设计师们提供了灵感，他们以保时捷Boxster为基础设计了一辆极致的民用跑车——保时捷 Le Mans Living Legend。

从设计上可以轻易辨认出保时捷 Le Mans Living Legend 的赛车血统：车辆的前、后机盖向着相反的方向展开，加油口则位于前机盖的正中央，（原版赛车当年的）发车序号醒目地贴满车身。

副驾驶车窗后方的大进气口昭示了发动机的不凡动力——一具有着嘹亮歌喉的八汽缸发动机。广义上看，这辆保时捷 Le Mans Living Legend可以被视作是如今保时捷718 Cayman GT4的前辈。

The Porsche 550 is mainly remembered for the purist Spyder. Its Le Mans career began with the first sports car from Stuttgart-Zuffenhausen with a closed roof specially designed for the racetrack. The 78 hp mid-engine sports car with a weight of around 550 kilograms made its debut at the 24 Hours of Le Mans in 1953. Behind the wheel were Helmut "Helm" Glöckler and Hans Herrmann. In 2016, the pioneering racing coupé with the crouching silhouette served Porsche's design team in Weissach as the inspiration for an extreme street sports car based on the Porsche Boxster.

It's really not hard to see the racetrack pedigree behind the design of the Porsche Le Mans Living Legend: The front and rear hoods open in opposite directions, refueling is via a central nozzle in the front, and the start numbers are emblazoned all around.

The large air inlets in the rear side windows indicate the nature of the engine used – an eight-cylinder model that generates an infernal sound. In the broadest sense, the fast-paced racing Porsche Le Mans Living Legend is a predecessor of today's Porsche 718 Cayman GT4.

保时捷Type 550 Spyder（原型车），1953 年勒芒赛场上的两辆原型车之一
Porsche Type 550 Spyder (prototype), one of two prototypes for the Le Mans race in 1953

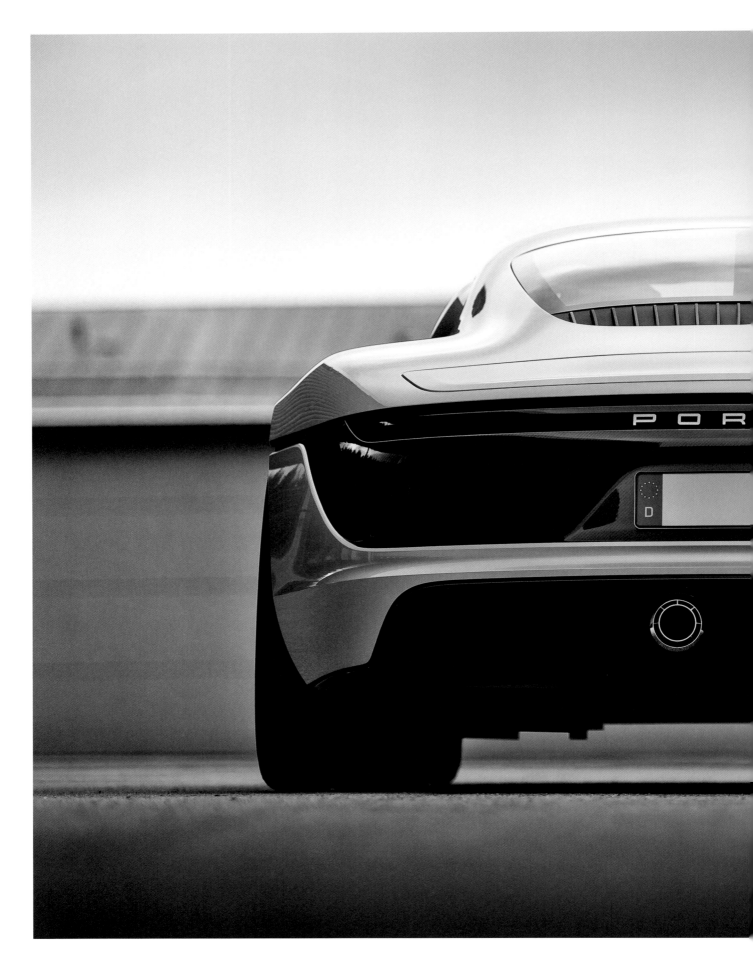

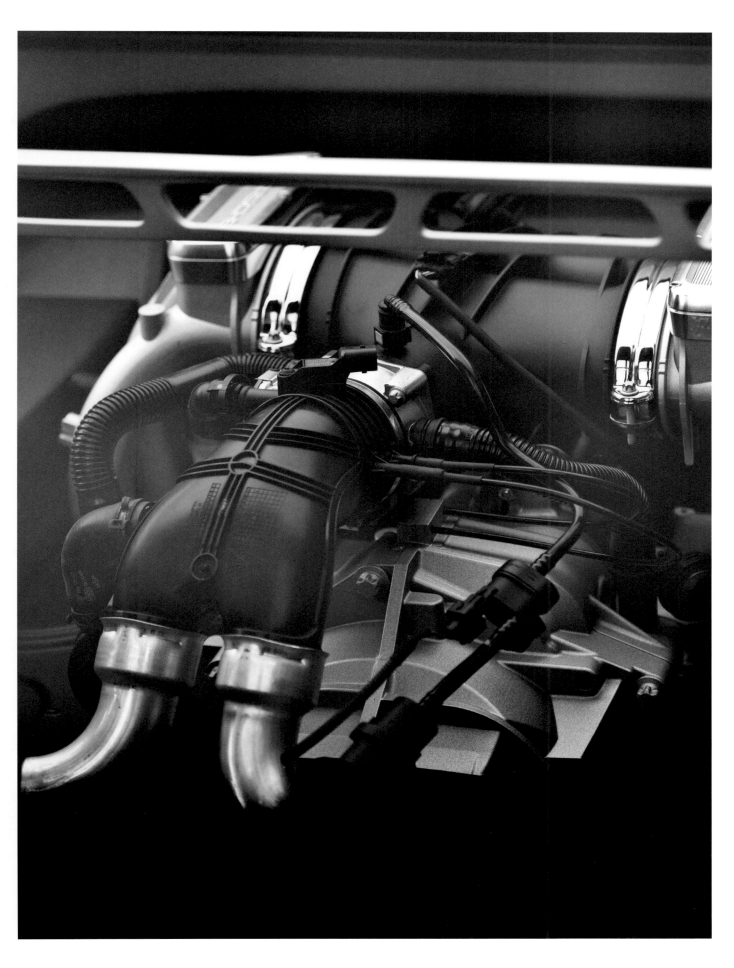

Porsche 911
Vision Safari

年份: 2012
Year: 2012

研发状态: 可行驶原型车
Stage of development
Drivable prototype

"我们坚信没有其他品牌可以像保时捷这样将跑车与越野元素结合得如此浑然天成。"首席设计师毛迈恪说道。早在20世纪70年代，保时捷911就在著名的东非拉力赛上展现出了惊人的越野能力。这项比赛穿越了肯尼亚沙漠的大部分地区，总赛程将近5000公里。1978年，保时捷厂队车手比约恩·瓦尔德戈德和小维克·普雷斯顿驾驶着抬高底盘、全面强化的带有马天尼涂装的保时捷911 SC Safari 赛车参赛。他们证明了采用风冷发动机的911不仅能在公路和赛道上一往无前，在沙漠中也是势不可挡。布满灰土的保时捷911 Safari 在非洲平原上漂移穿过水坑和泥沼的画面令人难忘。

因此，2012年，保时捷设计团队决定用当代的重新诠释向这部传奇越野赛车致敬。保时捷911 Vision Safari 以991代的911为基础打造，升高了底盘，轮拱被加强，还有着巨大的前保险杠和带有赛车座椅与防滚架的竞技化座舱，这是对历史上拉力车型的忠实致敬。设计师们甚至在座椅后方加入了风扇，用以在炎热赛段冷却头盔。

这辆911 Vision Safari 在非洲之外的首次亮相是在魏斯阿赫测试场的砂石路面上，这里通常是用来检验保时捷Cayenne 和 Macan 越野能力的场地。当设计老大毛迈恪回忆起他首次坐在副驾驶感受这辆拥有更柔和调校的911 Safari 时说了一句话："我很少有如此享受的时刻！"

"We believe that no other car brand can combine sports car and off-road characteristics as credibly as Porsche," says Head of Design Michael Mauer. As early as the 1970s, the Porsche 911 demonstrated its amazing off-road capabilities at the legendary East African Safari Rally. The race crossed a large part of the Kenyan desert, covering almost 5,000 kilometers. In 1978 Porsche works drivers Björn Waldegård and Vic Preston Jr. were right at the front of the pack with their jacked up, completely reinforced Porsche 911 SC Safari with the characteristic Martini stripes. They proved that the air-cooled 911 was almost unstoppable, not just on highways and racetracks, but also in the desert. The pictures of the dust-covered Porsche 911 Safari on the African plains and drifting through watering holes and mud pools are quite unforgettable.

That's why the Porsche design team decided to pay tribute to the legendary off-road athlete with a contemporary reinterpretation in 2012. The Porsche 911 Vision Safari was based on the 991 generation of the 911. With its raised chassis, reinforced wheel arches, massive bumpers and a spartan rally cockpit with racing seats and roll bars, it is a faithful homage to the historical rally model. The designers have even included a helmet rack on the fan wheel behind the seats to cool the helmet down between particularly heated stages.

The Porsche 911 Vision Safari made its maiden voyage "out of Africa" on the gravel track of the Weissach proving ground, where the Porsche Cayenne und Macan usually demonstrate their off-road capabilities. Design boss Michael Mauer was in the passenger seat during the first drift in the softly tuned Safari 911 and remembers fondly: "I've rarely enjoyed myself so much!"

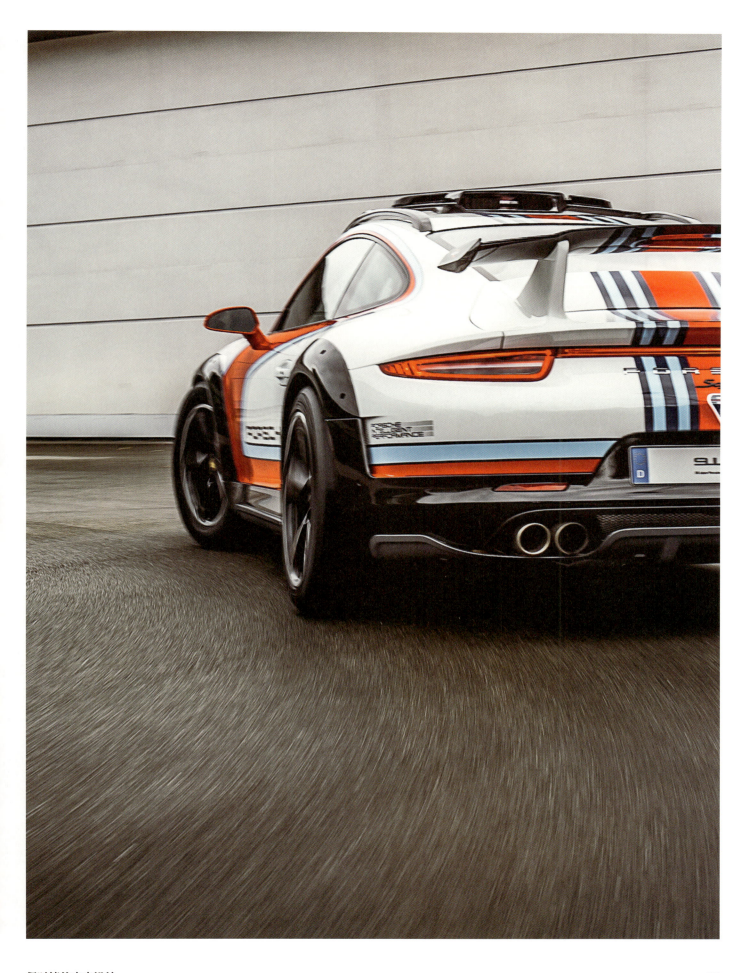

1978年的东非拉力赛上，911 SC 3.0 "Safari"
East African Safari Rallye 1978, 911 SC 3.0 "Safari"

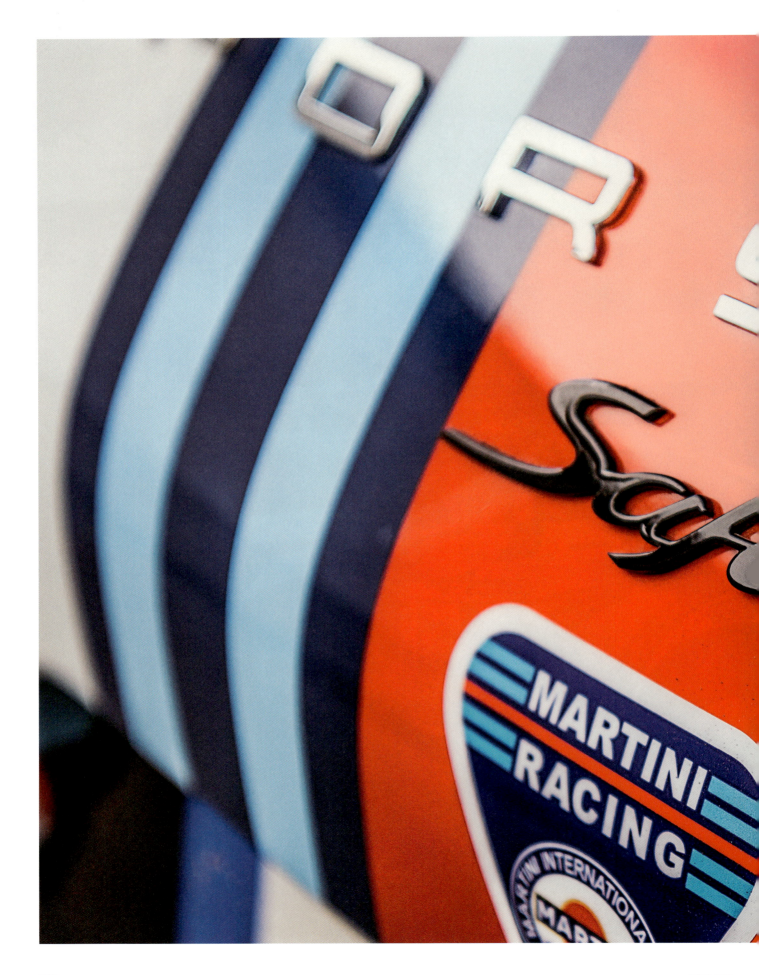

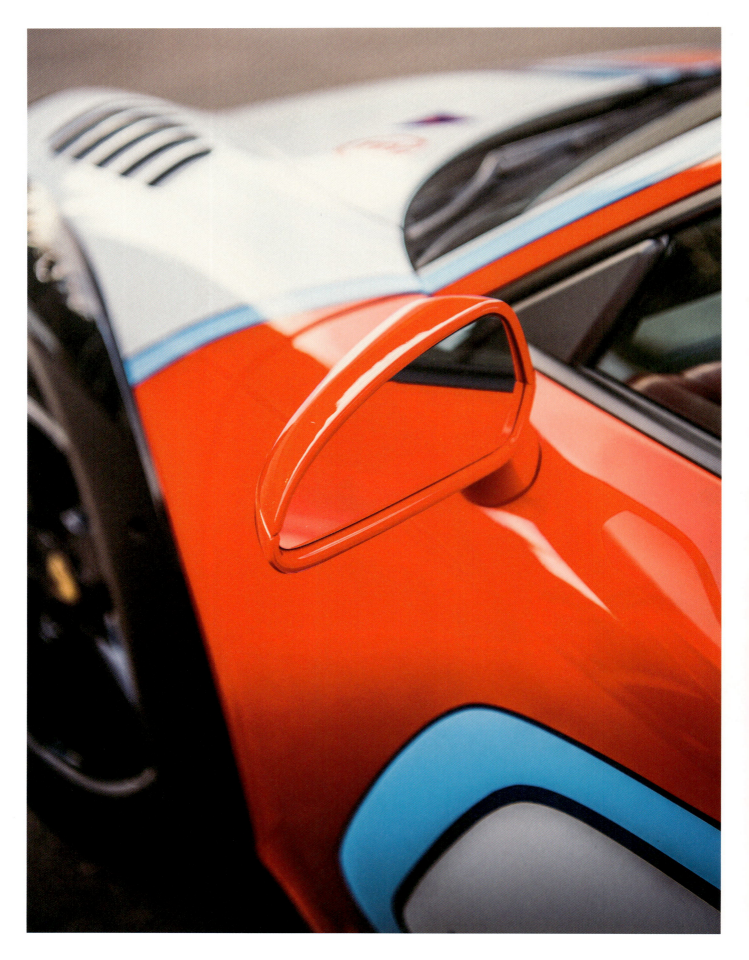

Porsche Macan Vision Safari

年份: 2013
Year: 2013

研发状态: 1 : 3硬质模型
Stage of development
Hard model, scale 1 : 3

对于保时捷 Macan 来说，时髦的都市道路才是它的归宿。但在它优雅的身躯之下有一个想去尘土与泥泞中释放越野能力的灵魂。

毕竟，这款成功的车型带有灵活的全轮驱动系统，运动化双离合变速器，自适应底盘能一键切换至越野模式。Macan 命中注定要去砂石路面和拉力赛道上去证明其多功能性。

它脱胎于保时捷历史上最知名的越野明星——保时捷911 Safari 和959巴黎—达喀尔拉力赛车，魏斯阿赫的设计团队为 Macan Vision Safari 换上了一套全地形轮胎。

作为一款具有更高离地间隙和许多强大附加功能的运动型三门车，这位越野运动员已经准备好离开柏油路，伴随着后视镜中的一阵烟尘去探索东非腹地或西伯利亚的大草原了。

The Porsche Macan is at home on the world's smartest boulevards. But under the elegant bodywork there is a real off-road miracle that is just waiting to be unleashed in dust and mud.

After all, this successful model has active all-wheel drive, a sporty dual clutch transmission (PDK) and an adaptive chassis that can be made fit for off-road terrain at the push of a button. The Macan is predestined to prove its versatility on gravel and rally slopes.

Loosely modelled on the brand's big off-road icons – the Porsche 911 Safari and the 959 Paris-Dakar – the design team in Weissach therefore fitted the Porsche Macan Vision Safari with a set of all-terrain wheels.

As a sporty three-door vehicle with increased ground clearance and many robust extras, the off-road athlete would be ready to leave the asphalt and explore the hinterlands of East Africa or the steppes of Siberia with a huge cloud of dust in the rear view mirror.

叛逆之躯
Little Rebels

Porsche 904 Living Legend
Porsche Vision 916
Porsche Vision Spyder

建筑大师路德维希·密斯·凡德罗那句"少即是多"的口号被奉为现代建筑学的奥义。而这句话也能概括保时捷赛车成功背后的故事。当其他厂商用堆砌性能的手法竞争时，保时捷的跑车与赛车更注重于灵巧轻量化的结构、功能的纯粹性、设计制造的独创性与适中的尺寸。在狭窄的赛道与蜿蜒的山路上，这套战术是难以战胜的。用现代的眼光打量保时捷历史上的经典车型，会发现一些车型的尺寸小到出乎意料——比如保时捷356、初代911、550 Spyder 和904等。

这也就不难理解为什么保时捷首席设计师毛迈恪与他的设计团队痴迷于设计身形紧凑却又性能强大的跑车——它们将驰骋在狭窄的山路和严苛的赛道上。那么，将这些纯粹的理念赋予21世纪的保时捷后会是什么样的？

设计中心里那些秘密的收藏品和近些年的概念研究告诉我们，答案可能非常宽泛。这也说明了，一辆为有运动追求的、灵敏触感的驾驶员服务的保时捷，将完美契合于品牌的产品阵列。

The "less is more" slogan of architect Ludwig Mies van der Rohe is regarded as the mantra of modern architecture. It could also be used as the title for the story of Porsche's sporting success. While other brands outdid each other in terms of excessive performance, sports cars and racing models from Porsche mostly garnered attention for their intelligent lightweight construction, purity of function, engineering ingenuity and modest dimensions. This combination was hard to beat, especially on narrow racetracks and steep winding roads. Many of the icons in the brand's history seem amazingly small to modern eyes – from the Porsche 356 to the first 911 and from the 550 to the 904.

It is therefore no surprise that Porsche's chief designer Michael Mauer and his team dream of a compact, lightweight and efficient sports car for narrow alpine roads and demanding circuits. But what might this purist sporty Porsche for the 21st century look like?

A glimpse at the secret collection at the Design Center and the concept studies of recent years reveals just how broad the answer might be. It also shows how well a compact Porsche for drivers with sporting ambitions and a sensitive touch would fit in with the brand universe.

Porsche 904
Living Legend

年份: 2013
Year: 2013

研发状态: 1:1硬质模型
Stage of development
Hard model, scale 1:1

有时候，优秀的理念会非常接近，在集团内部就会出现这样的例子。大众自2002年起便开始研制百公里油耗低至1升的汽车，2014年他们终于以小批量形式推出了大众 XL1。这项研究激起了保时捷设计工作室的兴趣，尤其是碳纤维单体壳底盘这个理念。轻巧紧凑的车身架构为研发超小型极简主义跑车提供了机会。设计团队开始尝试众多不同的车身造型，出乎所有人意料的是，定稿的车身尺寸、比例与博物馆里的一辆轻量化传奇赛车十分接近，那就是保时捷904。

定稿的是一款非常紧凑且高效的中置发动机跑车。它低矮的座舱和雕塑般的轮拱，无疑再现了1963年的保时捷904 Carrera GTS 的设计精髓，使其在当下重生。为这辆仅重900公斤的保时捷904 Living Legend 提供动力的，极有可能是一具加大马力的 V 型双缸摩托车发动机。

Sometimes good ideas are very close – for example within your own corporate family. Volkswagen had been conducting research into an economical one-liter car since 2002, and in 2014 the concept was launched as a small series in the form of the VW XL1. The study aroused interest in the Porsche Design Studio in particular for its carbon monocoque chassis. The light and compact vehicle architecture offered the opportunity to develop a radically small and minimalist sports car. The design team started experimenting with various body shapes. Much to everyone's surprise, the car that resulted was very similar in proportions and dimensions to one of the lightweight racing legends found in the works museum, the Porsche 904.

The result was an amazingly compact and efficient mid-engine sports car. With its crouched cockpit and sculptural wheel arches, it confidently brought the purist design idea of the legendary Porsche Carrera GTS from 1963 bang up to date. The engine used for the barely 900 kilo Porsche 904 Living Legend might have been a souped-up V2 motorcycle engine.

1963 年的 904 (001)，首次配备后缘，电机散热格栅尚未成为标准配置
Type 904 (001) from 1963 ; First implementation of the rear edge, motor cooling grille not yet standard

见所未见

Porsche
Vision 916

年份: 2016
Year: 2016

研发状态: 1:3油泥模型
Stage of development
Clay model, scale 1:3

当代最简约的保时捷会是什么样子？一名设计部的实习生用这款小而美的概念车回答了这个问题。为这辆灰蓝色概念车提供造型灵感的是紧凑的保时捷916，一款在20世纪70年代早期研发但从未投产的原型车。

保时捷 Vision 916 有四个轮毂电机，纯电力驱动，据称这也是向费迪南德·保时捷于1900年设计的洛纳－保时捷四轮驱动电动赛车的一次致敬。结合了轻量化技术，这款极简跑车保证了极大的驾驶乐趣。仿佛时刻准备着去大格洛克纳山或者斯泰尔维奥国家公园最蜿蜒的山路上一展身手，就如同当年保时捷356与911的首部原型车那样。

Just how minimalist can a modern-day Porsche be? An intern from the design team answered this question with this small and attractive vehicle concept. The stylistic inspiration for the powder blue study was the compact Porsche 916, which was developed as a prototype in the early 1970s, but never went into series production.

The Porsche Vision 916 is powered purely electrically by four wheel hub motors – a homage to the first Lohner-Porsche racing car with all-wheel drive, which automobile designer Ferdinand Porsche developed back in 1900. In combination with the low weight, the technology of the minimalist sports car promised great driving pleasure. It was crying out to be tested on the alpine pass roads of the Großglockner or Stilfserjoch – just like the first prototypes of the Porsche 356 and 911.

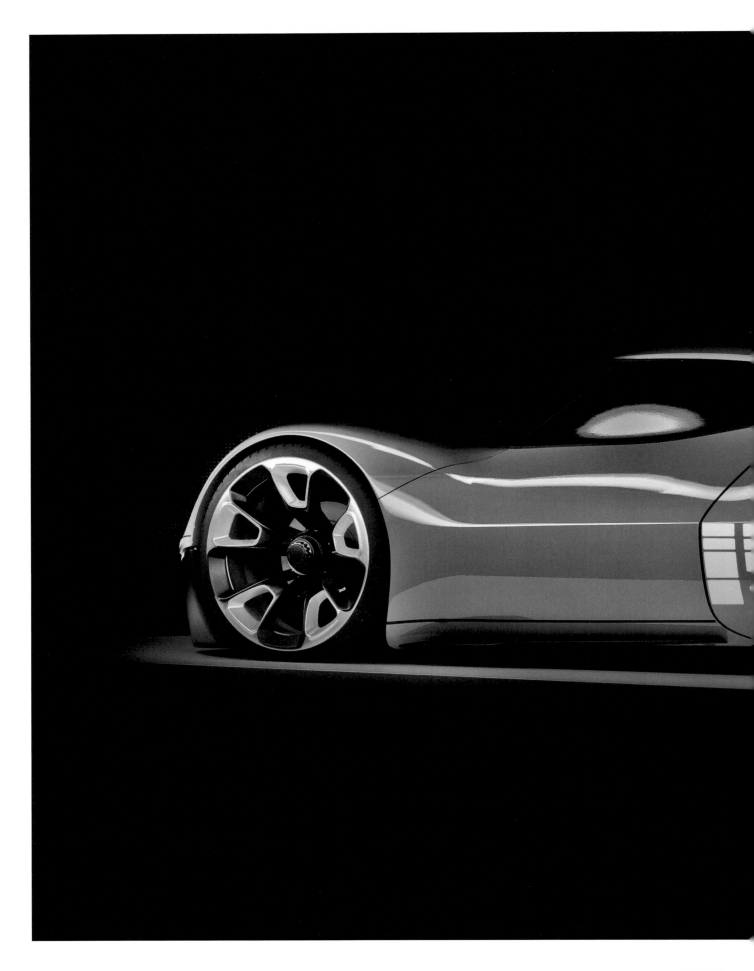

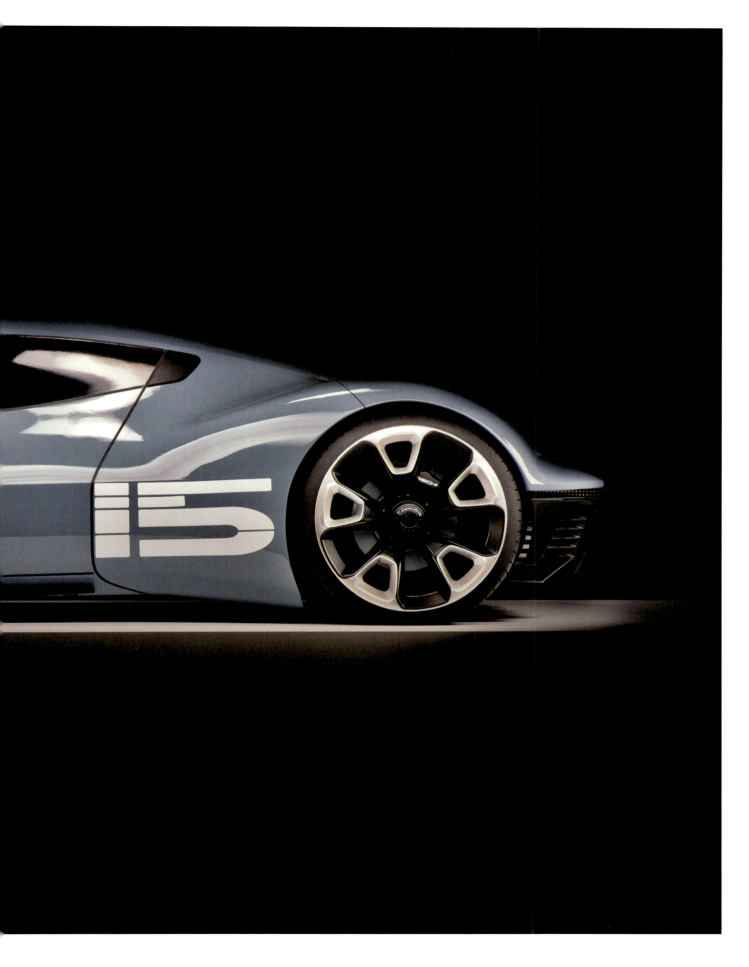

Porsche
Vision Spyder

年份: 2019
Year: 2019

研发状态: 1∶1硬质模型
Stage of development
Hard model, scale 1∶1

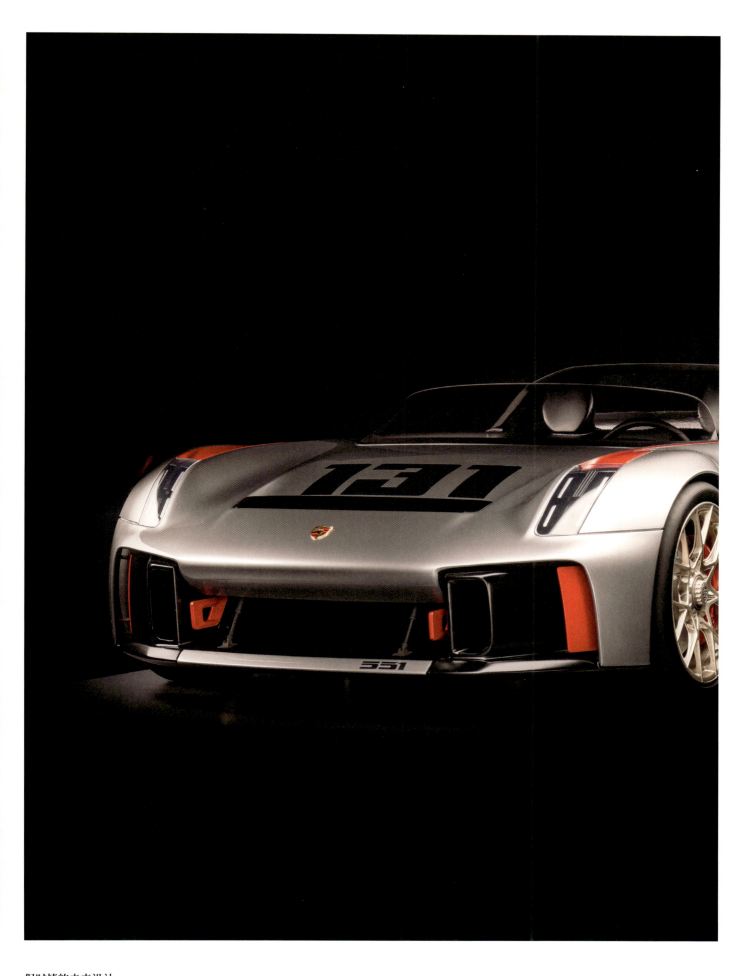

真正的叛逆是不需要理由的，詹姆斯·迪恩是保时捷历史上的伟大英雄之一。他那辆被称作"小混蛋"的银色保时捷550 Spyder 被我们怀念至今。不过，这辆 Vision Spyder 并不仅仅是设计团队向詹姆斯·迪恩及其跑车致敬的作品。保时捷550 Spyder 还在体积、尺度和设计元素方面提供了进一步的灵感。1954年，汉斯·赫尔曼就曾驾驶着赛车在传奇的泛美公路赛上从北到南穿越了整个墨西哥，行程近3000公里，最终取得了组别第一、全场第三的傲人战绩。

这款紧凑型跑车采用简洁的驾驶舱，中置发动机上方有扁平散热器格栅，后部有红色赛车条纹和造型低调的尾鳍设计，明显能让人联想到那辆泛美公路赛赛车。与此同时，这项研究进一步促进了带有内燃机的保时捷跑车设计特征的发展：前大灯的垂直布置和实用的空气动力学组件，例如有尖角的防滚架，这些都融入了保时捷的设计语言。

The eternal rebel without a cause, James Dean is one of the great heroes of Porsche history. His silver Porsche 550 Spyder, fondly nicknamed the "Little Bastard", has remained in our collective memories to this day. However, the Porsche Vision Spyder is not just the design team's homage to James Dean and his sports car. The Porsche 550 Spyder served as a further source of inspiration for the volumes, dimensions and formal design elements. In 1954, Hans Herrmann drove the racing car more than 3,000 kilometers from north to south through Mexico in the legendary Carrera Panamericana race, clinching a class win and third place overall for Porsche.

With its spartan cockpit, flat radiator grille over the midengine, red racing stripes and modest fins at the rear, the compact sports car is clearly reminiscent of the Carrera Panamericana racing car. At the same time, the study served as a further development of the design identity for Porsche sports cars with combustion engines: The vertical arrangement of the headlights to the front and the functional aero-dynamic elements, such as the angular roll bar, could thus be incorporated into Porsche's design language.

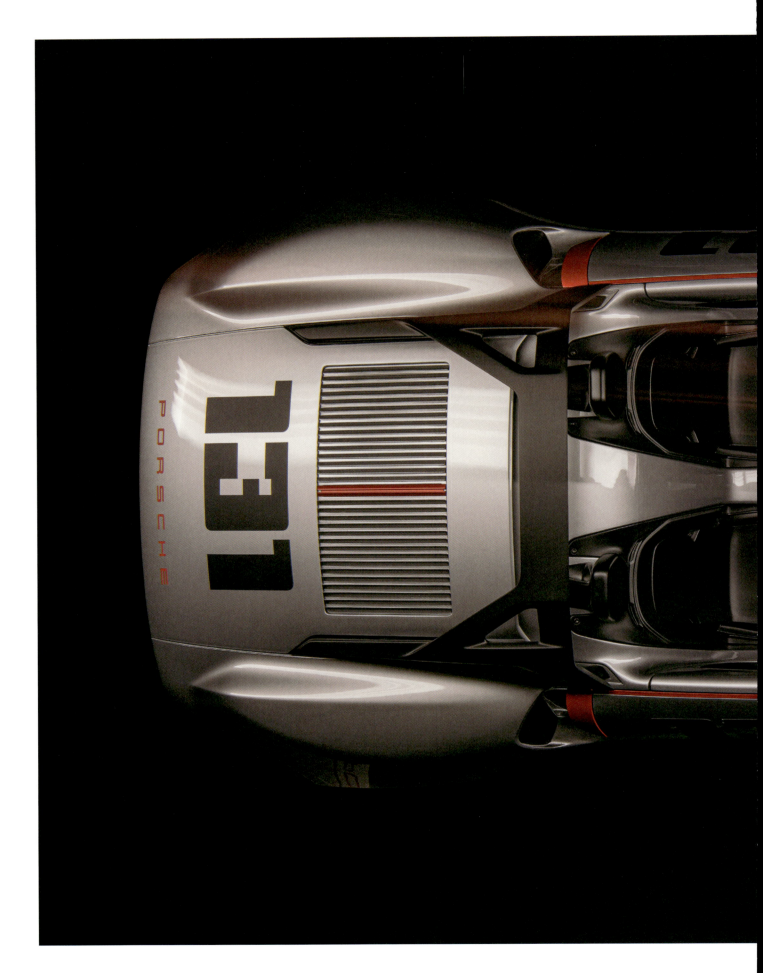

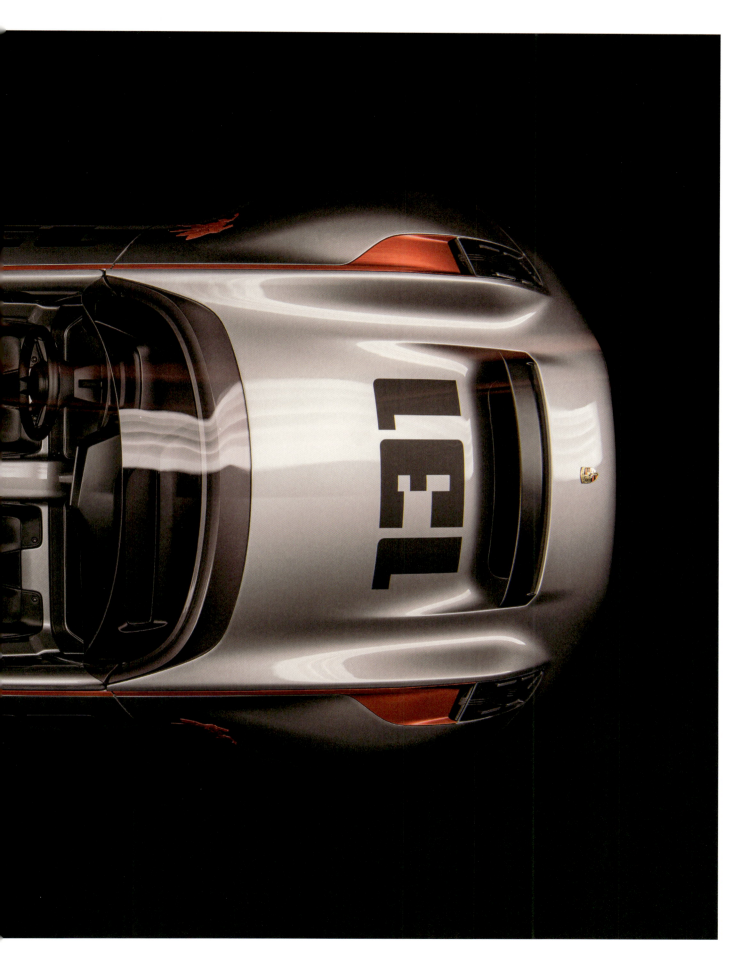

1956年的赛百灵12小时耐力赛上，杰克·麦卡菲和皮特·洛夫利驾驶的 43 号保时捷 550 Spyder
12 hours of Sebring, 1956: Jack McAfee and Pete Lovely in the #43 Porsche 550 Spyder

保时捷的未来设计

速度之魂
Hypercars

Porsche 919 Street
Porsche 917 Living Legend
Porsche 906 Living Legend
Porsche Vision 918
Porsche Vision E
Porsche Vision 920

哪些车最能定义保时捷? 在过去, 那些极致、最追求速度的代表品牌非凡技术的旗舰跑车会引起人们注意。保时捷904 Carrera GTS、959、911 GT1、Carrera GT 和918 Spyder 等, 这些如雷贯耳的大名让全世界的人们渴望拥有保时捷。在魏斯阿赫的设计中心, 人们已经开始畅想下一代的保时捷旗舰公路车型会是什么样子了。

从服务绅士车手的勒芒赛车到基于电动方程式的限量版单座车型, 几乎没有比这些激进的车型更令人兴奋的了。还记得费利·保时捷曾经说过什么吗? "世界上最后一辆被制造出来的汽车将会是跑车。"如果这位伟大的设计师和企业家今天还活着, 他可能会在这句话的末尾加上"或超级跑车"。

Which cars will one day shape our image of a Porsche? In the past, it was often the particularly extreme and fast sports cars that drew attention to the brand as flagships for technological prowess. The Porsche 904 Carrera GTS, the 959, 911 GT1, the Carrera GT and the 918 Spyder – all of these names made people the world over dream of owning a Porsche. At the Design Center in Weissach, people are already asking what the next generation of the ultimate Porsche sports car for the road might look like.

From Le Mans race cars for gentleman drivers to limited edition single-seater models based on Formula E – automobiles could hardly be more electrifying than these radical visions. What was it Ferry Porsche once said? "The last car ever built will be a sports car." If the great designer and entrepreneur were still alive today, he'd probably add the words "or hypercar" to that statement.

Porsche
919 Street

年份: 2017
Year: 2017

研发状态: 1:1硬质模型
Stage of development
Hard model, scale 1:1

它是21世纪最为迅猛也最为成功的赛车之一，也是保时捷赛车成功史上的新篇章：保时捷919 Hybrid在勒芒24小时耐力赛2015—2017赛季成功斩获了三连冠。2018年，赛车手蒂莫·伯恩哈德驾驶着一辆"进化版"的勒芒冠军赛车以5分19秒55的成绩刷新了纽博格林北环赛道的最快圈速。这是一个全新的赛道纪录。在保时捷宣布将退出勒芒原型车组别的竞争后，毛迈恪与他的团队有了一个新想法：创造一款限量版的保时捷919 Hybrid为这款大获成功的赛车献礼。

保时捷919街道版基于现有的科技打造，企图让业余车手也能享受LMP1勒芒原型车澎湃的驾驶激情。在这辆车的外壳下，是碳纤维单体车身和与在勒芒获胜的那辆919 Hybrid赛车相同的900马力混合动力系统。这辆车的车身尺寸与轴距都和勒芒赛车一致。（保时捷内部）曾一度认为可以制造一款无需上路许可的限量版定制赛车。然而高性能的赛车技术格外复杂——单是启动勒芒原型车的发动机便需要一组专业赛车技师花费45分钟，公司不得不组建了一支"飞行医生"派往全球赛道。因此，这个将勒芒冠军车推广给绅士车手的计划就成了一个美丽的白日梦。

It is one of the fastest and most successful racing cars of the 21st century and the latest chapter in the success story behind motorsport at Porsche: The Porsche 919 Hybrid took the title in the 24 Hours of Le Mans three times in a row, from 2015 to 2017. In 2018, racing driver Timo Bernhard completed a lap of the Nürburg-ring Nordschleife in an evolved version of the Le Mans winning car in just 5 minutes 19.55 seconds. This was a new track record. After Porsche announced its withdrawal from LMP1 racing, a new idea arose among the design team under Michael Mauer in Weissach: to crown the success story with a limited special edition of the Porsche 919 Hybrid for the racetrack.

The Porsche 919 Street was created using existing technology and promised to open up the overwhelming driving experience of the LMP1 racing car possible to amateur drivers too. Under the outer shell are the carbon monocoque and the 900 hp hybrid racing engine that brought the Porsche 919 victory at Le Mans. The dimensions and wheelbase were also identical with the race car. For a short time it seemed possible to build a customer vehicle in limited numbers without road traffic certification. But the high-performance racing technology was complex – it took a team of mechanics around 45 minutes just to start the LMP1 engine. The company would have had to dispatch a team of "flying doctors" to racetracks all over the world. Thus, the idea of a Le Mans winner for gentleman drivers remains just a beautiful pipe dream for the time being.

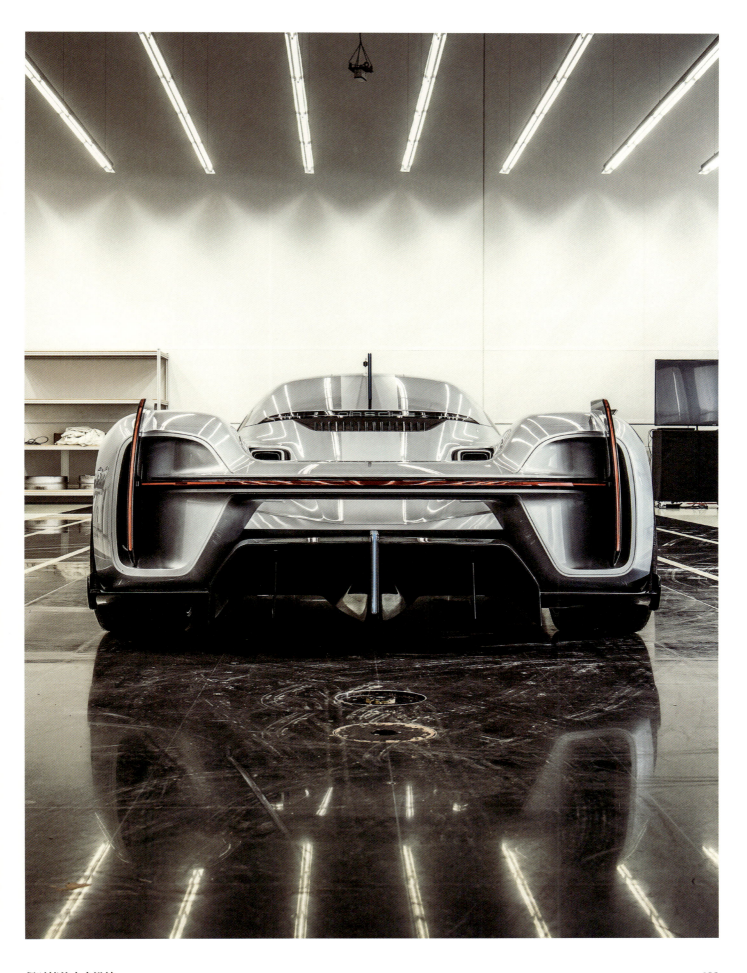

2015年在勒芒, 919 Hybrid 与蒂莫·伯恩哈德、马克·韦伯和布伦登·哈特利
Le Mans 2015, 919 Hybrid with Timo Bernhard, Mark Webber and Brendon Hartley

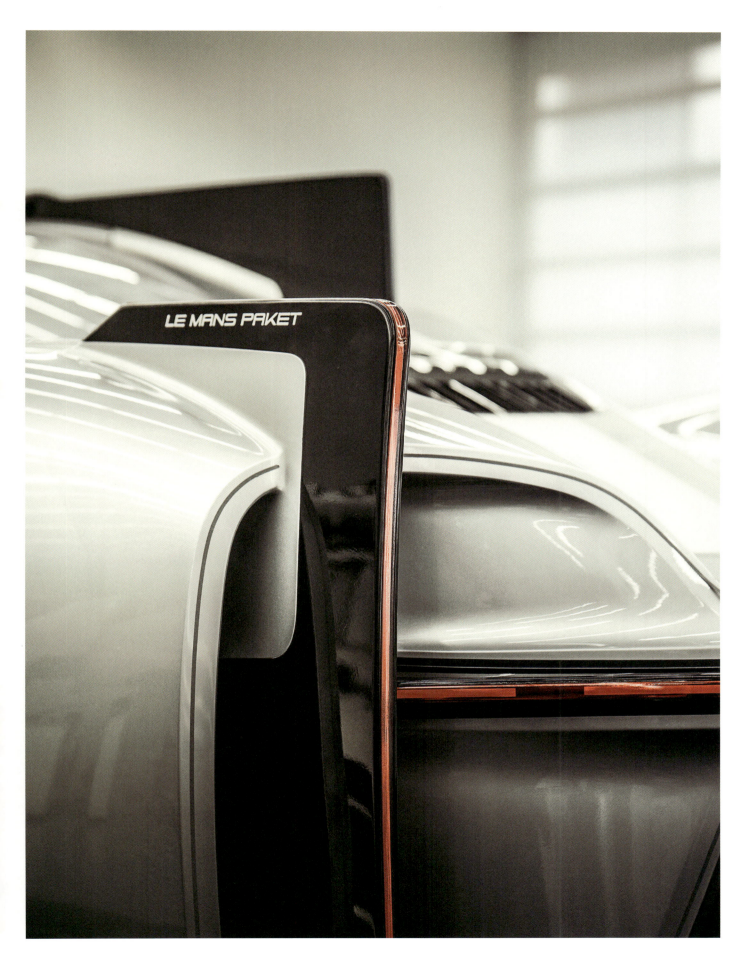

Porsche 917
Living Legend

年份: 2013
Year: 2013

研发状态: 1∶1油泥模型
Stage of development
Clay model, scale 1∶1

保时捷已经19次摘得勒芒24小时耐力赛的桂冠。而身披萨尔茨堡红白涂装的保时捷917KH赛车在品牌历史中有着非常特殊的地位：1970年夏天，汉斯·赫尔曼和理查德·艾特伍德驾驶着这辆赛车为保时捷在萨特赛道拿下了首个总成绩冠军。为了纪念保时捷回归勒芒原型车组别，魏斯阿赫的设计团队在2013年设计了一款现代版的保时捷917。6个月后，一个1：1的油泥模型带着让"活着的传奇"跟上时代步伐的使命诞生了。

"作为一款与过去有着明显呼应的新型超级跑车，这项设计是为了清晰地强调与保时捷917的联系。"毛迈恪解释道。发动机和底盘架构的技术基础由保时捷918 Spyder 提供。有着显著延展的轮拱，向前伸得更远的驾驶舱，看似无穷无尽的车尾和红白相间的赛车条纹，这台概念车显然让人想起1970年的获胜赛车。对毛迈恪来说还有一个设计元素堪称关键："从保时捷906到918，保时捷的超级跑车总是给你一种感觉，仿佛你就坐在高耸轮拱之间的道路上。我们想要强调这一点。"

2019年，为纪念保时捷917诞生50周年，这辆超跑愿景之车在保时捷博物馆纪念特展"速度之色"上首次与公众见面。

Porsche has already won the 24 Hours of Le Mans a solid 19 times. And yet the Porsche 917 KH in the red and white livery of Porsche Salzburg has a very special place in the brand's history: Behind the wheel, Hans Herrmann and Richard Attwood achieved their first overall victory for Porsche at the Circuit de la Sarthe in the summer of 1970. To mark the return of Porsche to the LMP1 class, the development team in Weissach developed a modern interpretation of the Porsche 917 in 2013. In six months, a 1:1 scale plasticine model was created with the intention of bringing the "living legend" up to date.

"The design was to clearly underline the link to the Porsche 917 – as a new Super Sports Car with clear echoes of the past," explains Michael Mauer. The technical basis for the engine and the architecture of the chassis was provided by the Porsche 918 Spyder. With its dramatically extended wheel arches, cockpit pulled far forward, a seemingly endless rear end and red and white racing trim, the concept study was clearly reminiscent of the winning car from 1970. There was another design element that was key for Michael Mauer: "From the Porsche 906 to the 918, Porsche's Super Sports Cars always give you the feeling that you are practically sitting on the road between the high wheel arches. We wanted to emphasize this even more."

To mark the 50th anniversary of the Porsche 917, the Super Sports Car vision 2019 was unveiled to the public for the first time at the "Colors of Speed" exhibition in the Porsche Museum.

1970 年，勒芒 24 小时耐力赛，汉斯·赫尔曼和理查德·艾特伍德驾驶23号 917 KH
24h of Le Mans, 1970: Hans Herrmann and Richard Attwood in the 917 KH Coupé #23

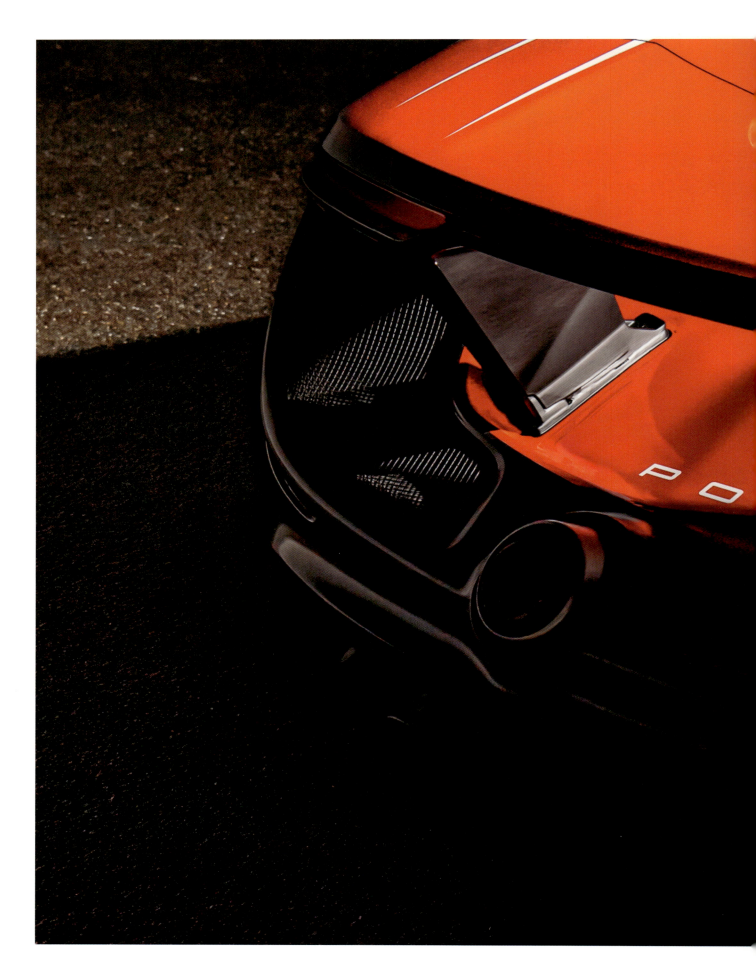

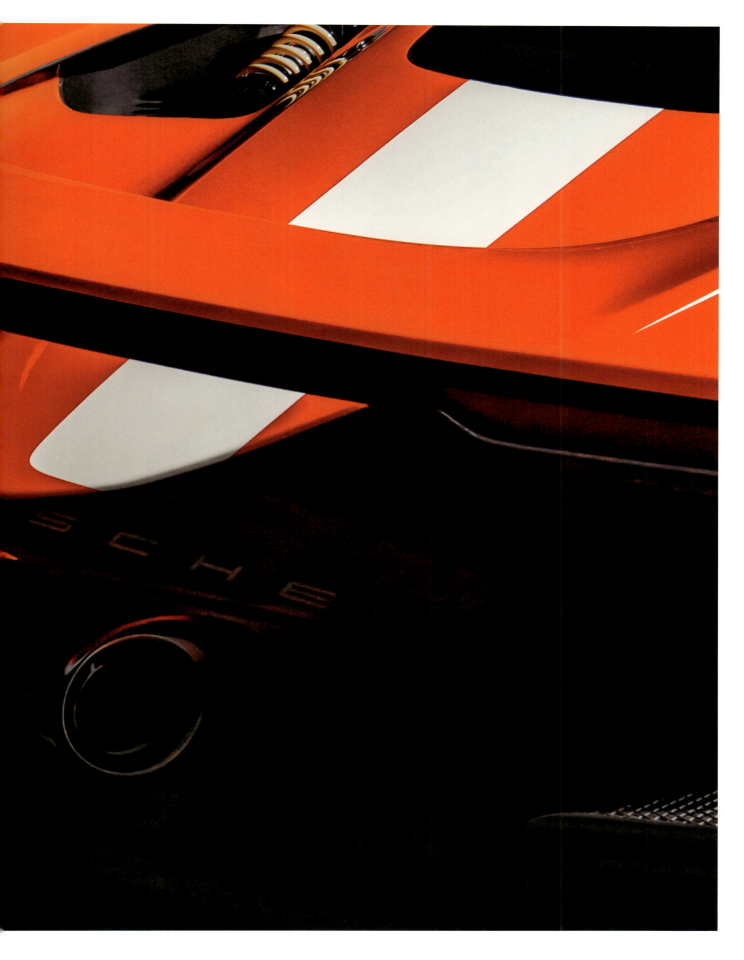

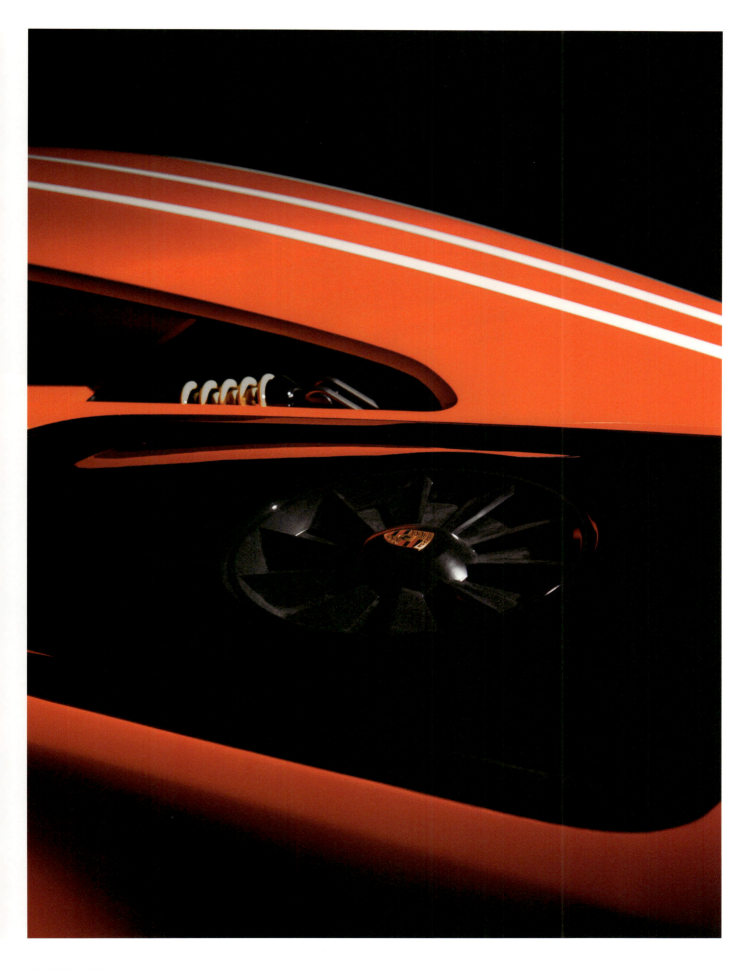

Porsche 906
Living Legend

年份: 2015
Year: 2015

研发状态: 1:3硬质模型
Stage of development
Hard model, scale 1:3

尽管设计团队正在其开放式设计项目中致力于未来汽车的开发，但保时捷的品牌历史始终是灵感的源泉。这辆超级跑车概念车显然参考了保时捷906的整体比例与车身设计。一方面，对比鲜明的红色发动机盖和前大灯的布置让人联想到那辆传奇的赛车及它在1966年塔格·佛罗热比赛上令人难忘的表现；同时，该研究充分利用这次机会在灯光和进气口之间建立起了风格十足的联系。

"这个项目的设计自由度很高，"毛迈恪解释道，"设计师不需要被已定义的产品标识特性所禁锢，这就是为什么车前灯演变成为位于前进气口中的未来光源。后来，当我们后来为未来电动车寻找一个合适的设计特征时，我们又回到了这些设计上。将车前灯简单地嵌入开口中而不用玻璃罩的激进想法对我们来说很恰当，我们正在逐渐接近这个理想中的理念。"

将保时捷906 Living Legend的车身呈现为好像两个模块挤压在一起的样子，也颇具创意——两片车身之间的间隙作为强大的中置发动机的进气口。毛迈恪认为这是一个核心设计特征。"当代超级跑车极端依赖空气动力学设计和各种开了洞的零件来应对导风的需求。"两个带有红色发光尾灯的陡峭垂直尾翼在车尾营造出了引人瞩目的效果。

Even though the design team is working on the development of the cars of the future in its open design projects, Porsche's brand history is always present as a source of inspiration. This vision of a Super Sports Car has obviously taken the Porsche 906 as its model for the proportions and body design. On the one hand, there is the front with its contrasting red hood and the arrangement of the main headlights, which are reminiscent of the legendary racing car and its unforgettable outing at the 1966 Targa Florio. At the same time, the study makes the most of the opportunities to create a stylistic link between the lights and the air inlets.

"The design process for visions like this is very free," explains Michael Mauer. "There is no need to get hung up on predefined product identity features. That's why the headlights have become futuristic light sources in air inlets. When we were later looking for a way to develop a special identity for our electric models, we returned yet again to these designs. The radical idea of simply integrating a light into an opening instead of using a glass cover seemed appropriate to us. We are getting closer to this ideal."

The idea of presenting the body of the Porsche 906 Living Legend as two elements that have been pushed together is also innovative – with the gap between the elements as a ventilation channel for a powerful mid-engine. Michael Mauer sees this as a central design feature. "Modern hypercars rely heavily on their aerodynamic design and pierced elements as a response to the enormous ventilation requirements." Two steeply inclined vertical fins with glowing red lights create a dramatic finish at the rear.

1966 年，纽博格林 1000 公里赛，罗伯特·邦杜兰特/保罗·霍金斯驾驶 17 号保时捷 Typ 906
1000 km race at the Nürburgring, 1966: Robert Bondurant/Paul Hawkins in the #17 Porsche Typ 906

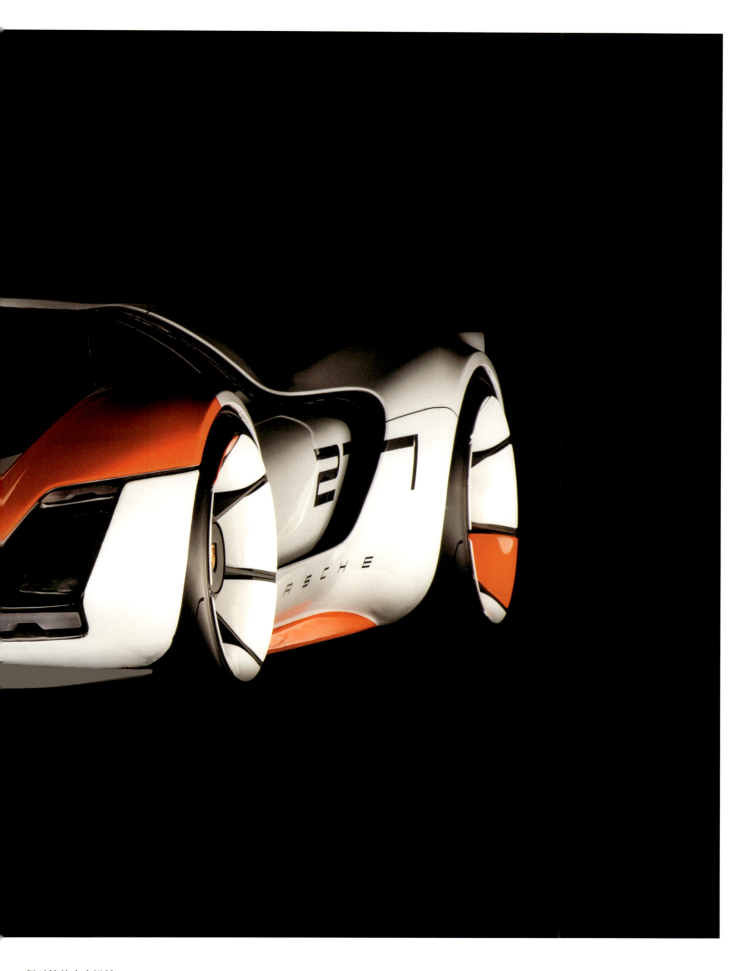

见所未见

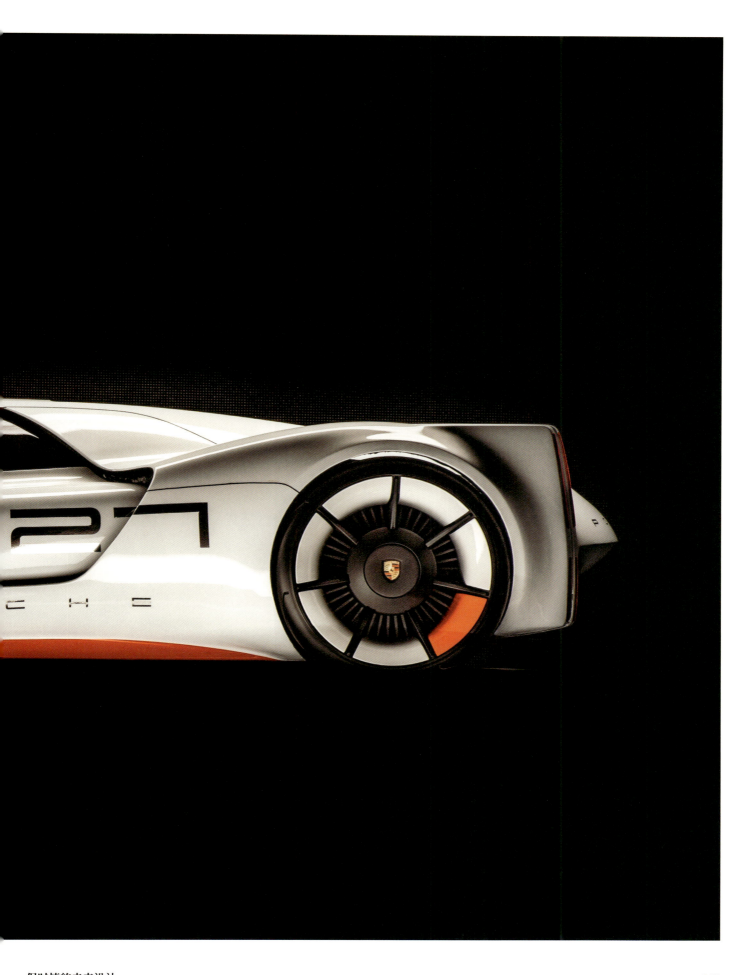

Porsche
Vision 918

年份: 2019
Year: 2019

研发状态: 1:3硬质模型
Stage of development
Hard model, scale 1:3

保时捷 918 Spyder 是其品牌赛车史上的里程碑之一。它于 2010 年作为一款引人入胜的展示车首次亮相，引导了混合动力车作为技术平台的战略，并以其全碳车身和全可变空气动力学为超级跑车设定了新标准。甚至在停产 5 年后，它依然是标杆之作。同时，918 Spyder 也是首辆在 7 分钟之内跑完纽博格林北环赛道的量产跑车。

这个独特的成功故事如何续写？在这个项目中，魏斯阿赫的设计团队专注于打造一款既能在赛道上，也能在公路上行驶的超级跑车，并在此过程中创造一个全新的、引人入胜的进化版保时捷 918。凭借先进的驱动和底盘技术，以及完美运用空气动力学设计的车身，保时捷 Vision 918 将成为魏斯阿赫最新一款超级跑车的终极变体。

The Porsche 918 Spyder is one of the sporting milestones in the history of the brand. It made its debut in 2010 as a fascinating show car, ushering in the strategy for the hybrid as a technology platform and setting new standards for Super Sports Cars with its full carbon body and fully variable aerodynamics. Even five years after production ended, it still remains a benchmark. The Porsche 918 Spyder was also the first production sports car to complete the Nürburgring Nordschleife circuit in less than seven minutes.

How can this unique success story continue? In this project, the design team in Weissach concentrated on the idea of a Super Sports Car that would be at home both on the racetrack and on the road – and in the process created a new, fascinating evolutionary stage for the Porsche 918. With advanced drive and chassis technology and a dramatically designed, aerodynamically perfected body, the Porsche Vision 918 would be the ultimate variation on the last Super Sports Car from Weissach.

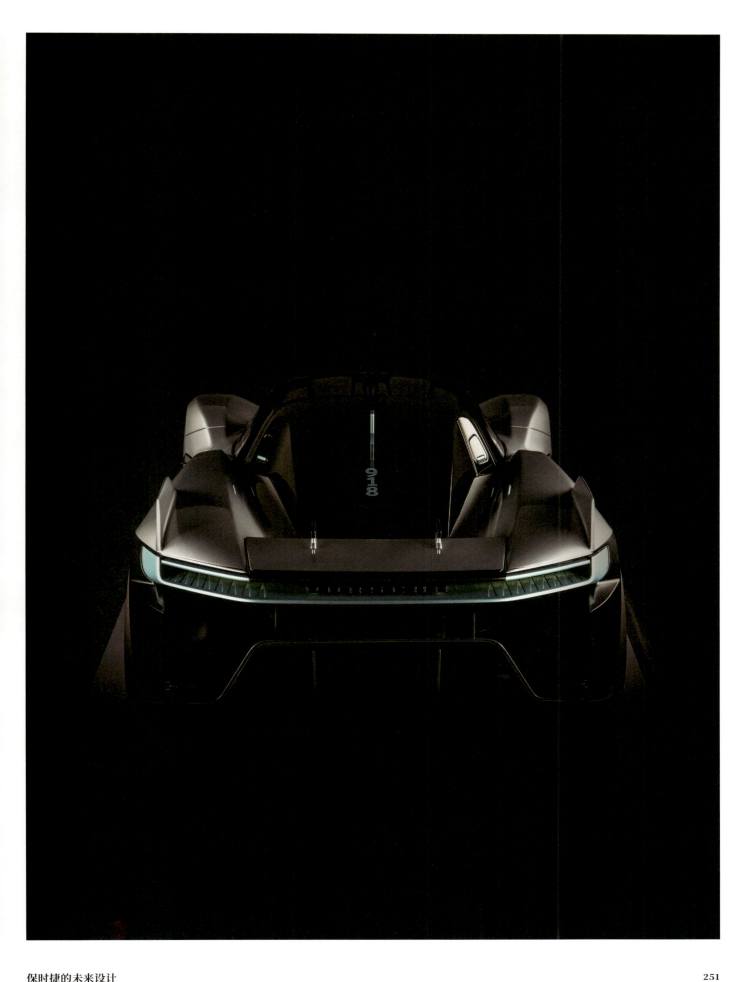

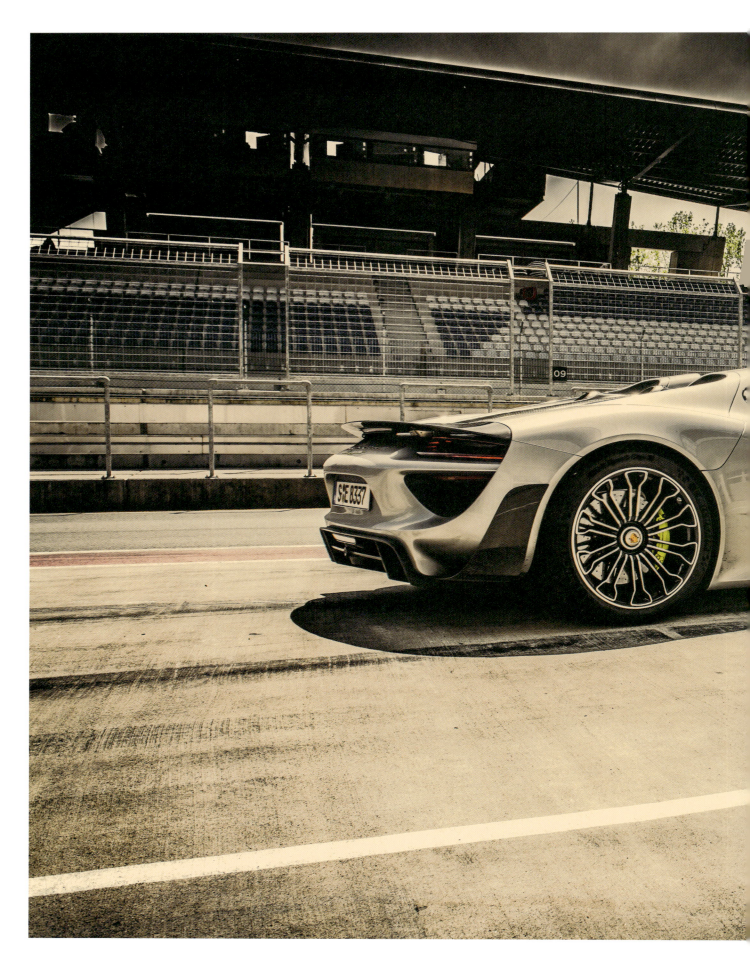

红牛赛道上的保时捷 918 Spyder，施皮尔贝格，奥地利
Porsche 918 Spyder at the Red Bull Ring in Spielberg, Austria

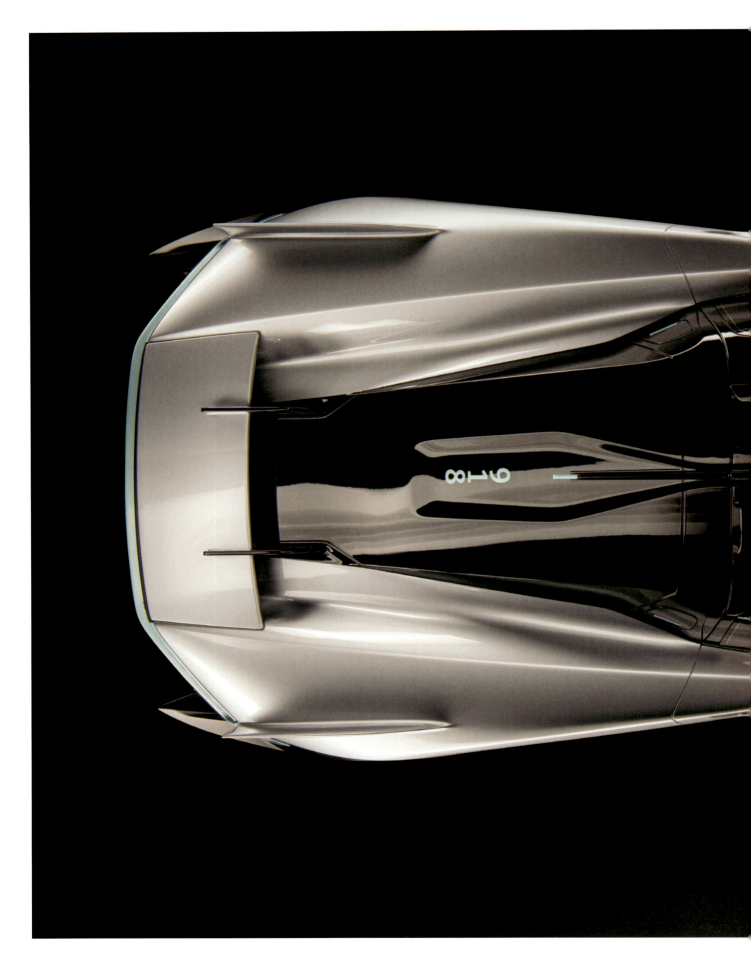

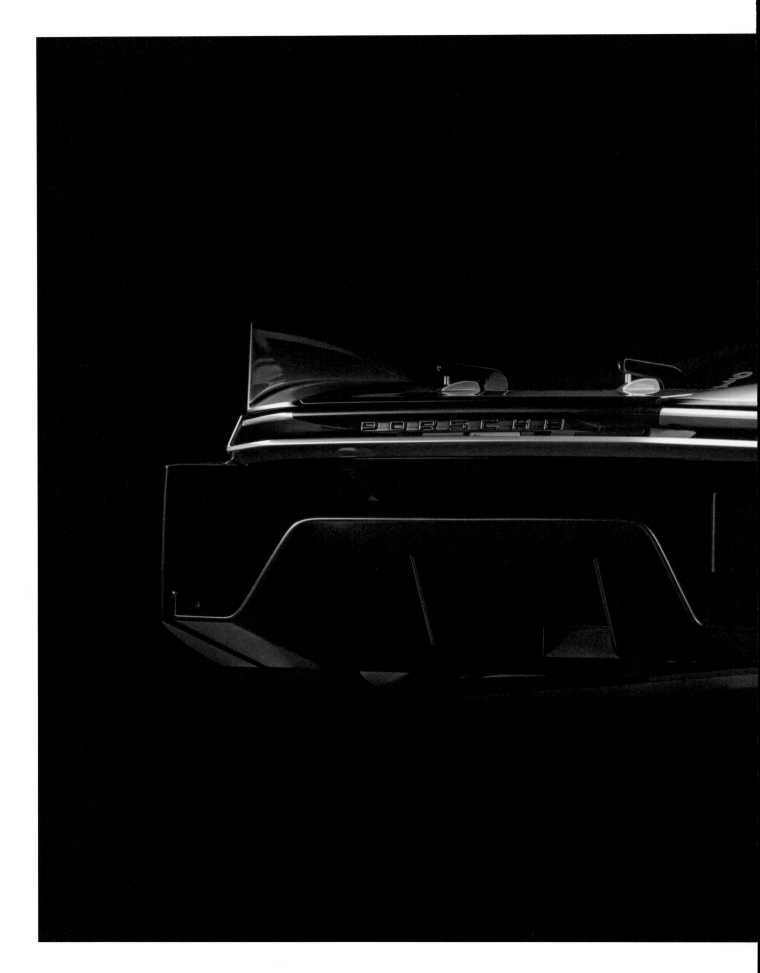

Porsche Vision E

年份: 2019
Year: 2019

研发状态: 1：3硬质模型
Stage of development
Hard model, scale 1：3

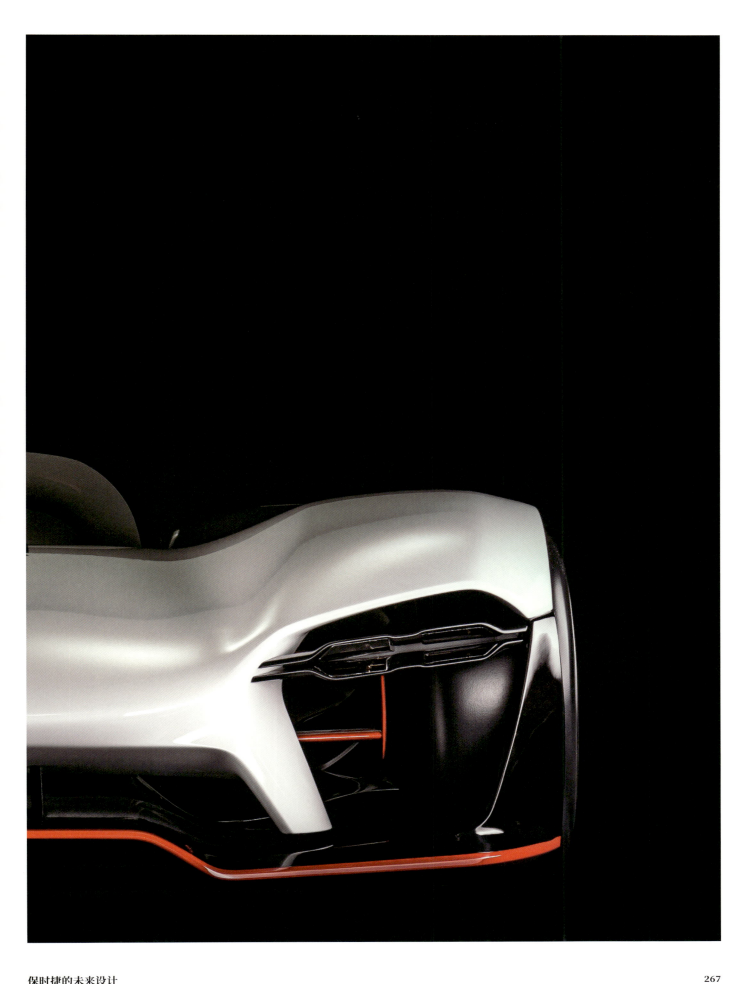

电动方程式或许是世界上最具创新性的汽车系列赛。在这里，未来的技术在最恶劣的条件下进行测试，将其推向极限并提高性能、效率和可持续性。保时捷也迎接了这个新的挑战，从2019年开始便参加了这个纯电动街道赛事。保时捷99X Electric 也加入了"魏斯阿赫制造"的创新赛车行列。独立开发的动力传动系统也成为未来纯电动赛车和公路跑车的基础。

这就是保时捷推广客户赛车运动的方式。这意味着为个人提供一辆在性能和驾驶动态方面尽可能接近现代电动方程式赛车的赛车。因此，保时捷 Vision Formula E 被设计为一款用于赛道的非常轻便的单座赛车。凭借居中的驾驶位和800伏技术，它将为私人车主提供其他车辆无法实现的驾驶体验。

Formula E is probably the most innovative race series in the world. This is where the technology of the future is tested under the toughest conditions, pushing it to the limit and enhancing performance, efficiency and sustainability. Porsche is also facing up to the new challenge and has been taking part in the fully electric road races since 2019. The Porsche 99X Electric joins the ranks of innovative racing cars "Made in Weissach". The independently developed drivetrain also served as the basis for future, purely electric racing and street sports cars.

This is how the idea of expanding customer motorsport developed at Porsche. This meant offering private individuals a vehicle for the racetrack that would come as close as possible to a modern Formula E racing car in terms of performance and driving dynamics. Hence, the Porsche Vision Formula E is designed as a radically lightweight, single-seat race car for the circuit. With its central seat position and 800 Volt technology, it would offer privateers an otherwise unattainable driving experience.

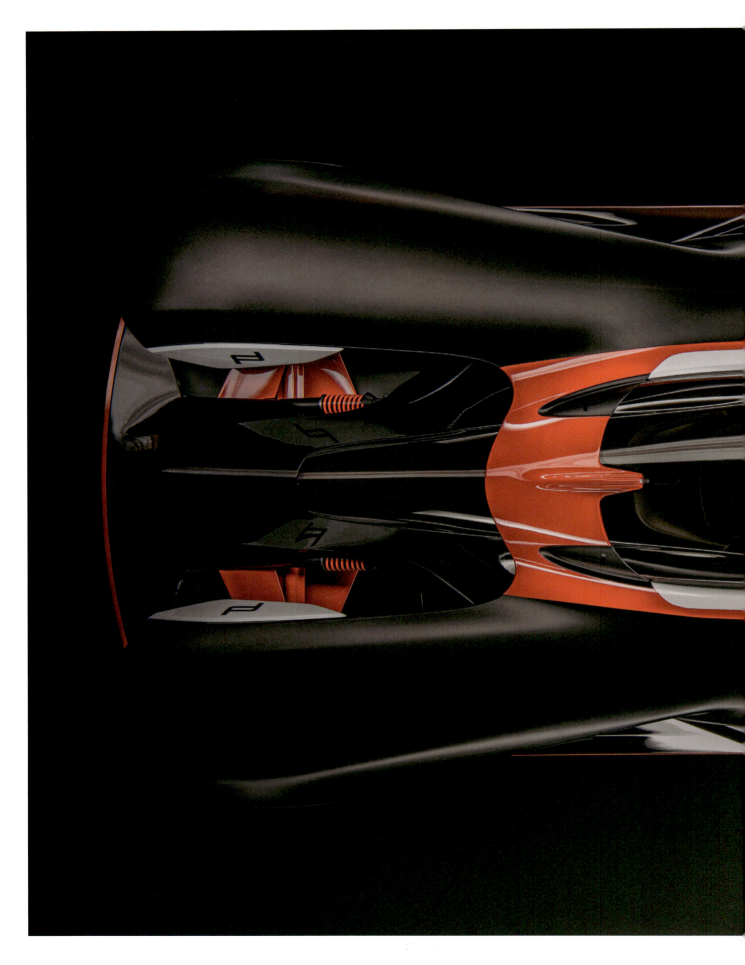

Porsche
Vision 920

年份: 2019
Year: 2019

研发状态: 1∶3硬质模型
Stage of development
Hard model, scale 1∶3

在保时捷，划分赛车与民用车的界限一直是不断变化的。这自然是勒芒24小时耐力赛的巨大成功赋予了品牌额外的明星品质。保时捷19次在萨尔特赛道上获胜——远超过任何其他制造商，最近的一次是在2015年至2017年间凭借919赛车获得了三连胜。即使在保时捷退出勒芒原型车组别之后，毛迈恪的设计团队仍然痴迷于"勒芒神话"，并尝试将赛车主题应用到客户赛车和街车上。

保时捷 Vision 920 被设计为一款超级公路跑车，或者是一款基于勒芒原型车并有可能成为客户赛车的车。设计师们特别关心的问题是，保时捷既有的设计语言如何与原型赛车功能强大又有明显美学印记的设计特征相结合。驾驶员坐在中央驾驶舱内。车身紧贴地面，如同漂浮在地面上，并具有许多较深的导风口。红白相间的保时捷 Vision 920 无疑是魏斯阿赫近年来开发的超级跑车中最极端的愿景之一。

The line dividing the racetrack from the street has always been fluid at Porsche. Naturally it is the great successes at the 24 Hours of Le Mans that have given the brand extra star quality. Porsche triumphed on the Circuit de la Sarthe 19 times – more often than any other manufacturer. Most recently, Porsche clinched three overall victories in a row with the 919 race car between 2015 and 2017. Even after Porsche withdrew from LMP1 sport, the design team under Michael Mauer remained fascinated by the "myth of Le Mans" and experimented with variations on the racing theme for customer sport and street use.

The Porsche Vision 920 was designed as a Super Sports Car for the road or a possible racing car for customer motorsports based on the LMP1 racing car. The designers were particularly concerned with the question of how the design language already established at Porsche could be combined with the highly functional, aesthetically impressive features of the prototype race cars. The driver sits in a central cockpit. The car body floats just above the ground and features a number of deep vents. The red and white Porsche Vision 920 is without doubt one of the most extreme visions of a Super Sports Car developed in Weissach in recent years.

见所未见

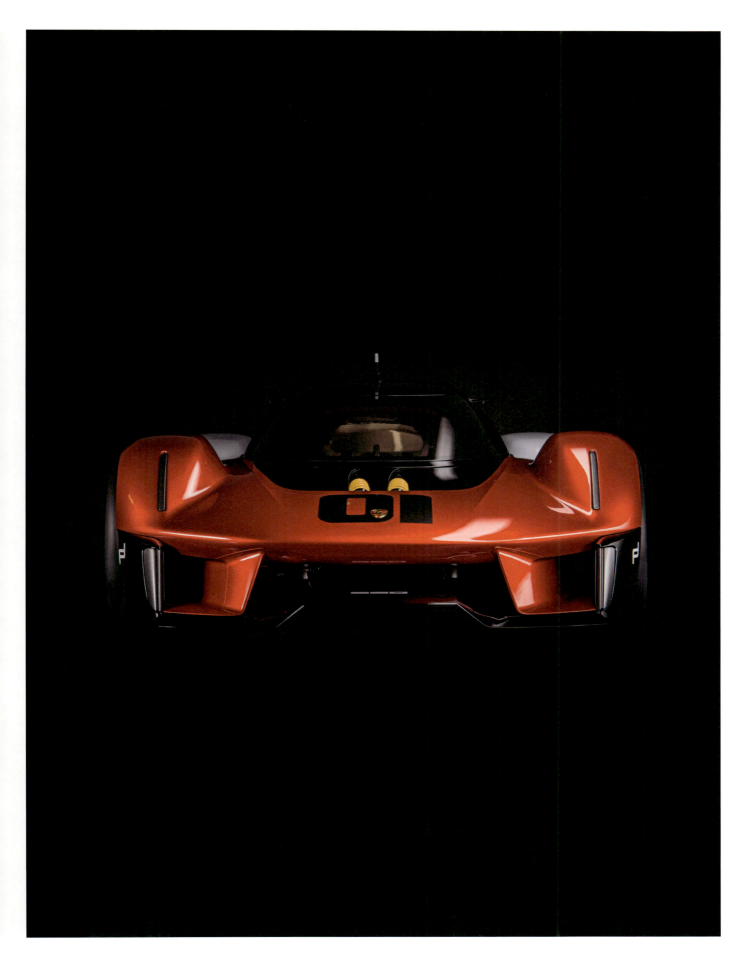

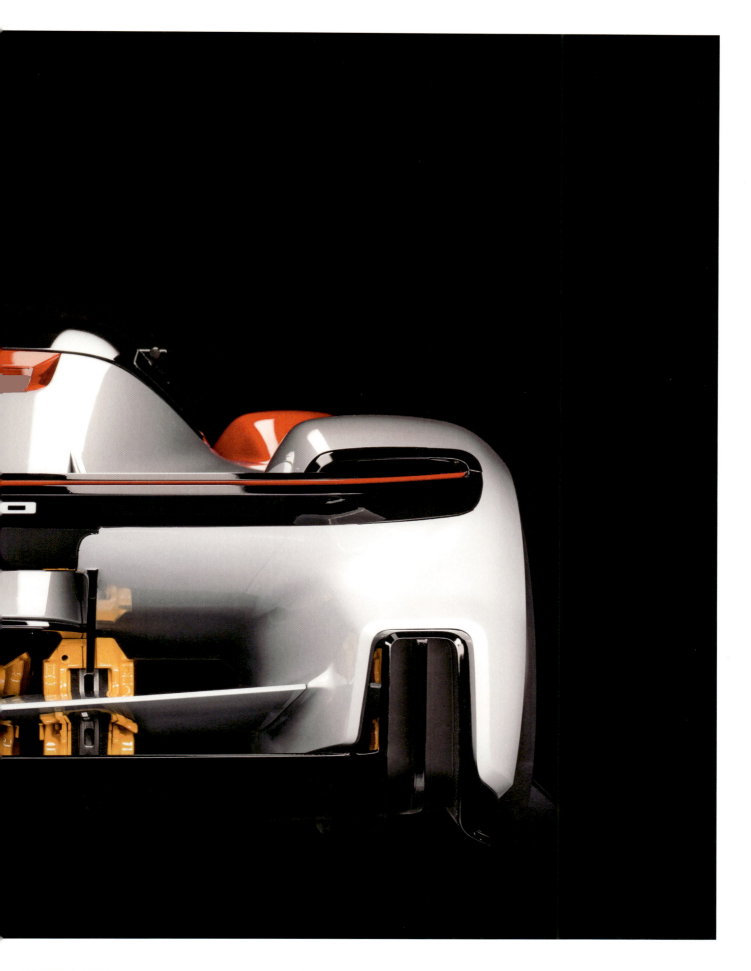

接下来会是?
What's Next?

Porsche Vision Turismo
Porsche Vision "Renndienst"

未来的保时捷是什么样的?哪些汽车类型可以成功补充品牌产品线?为了给这些问题找到真正意义上新颖、创新的答案,毛迈恪和他的设计团队不得不一次又一次地离开他们的舒适区,勇敢地跃入未知领域。这是他们定义新机会、激发思维过程并找到方向的唯一途径。这就是为何他们在开发全新量产汽车这样高度复杂的过程中,能够激发出那些惊人的巧合,而这些巧合有时也起着非常关键的作用。

What will the Porsche of tomorrow look like? And which automobile types could successfully complement the brand portfolio? In an effort to find really new and innovative answers to these questions, Michael Mauer and his design team have to leave their comfort zone time and again, daring to leap into the unknown. This is the only way for them to define new opportunities, stimulate thought processes and offer a guiding light. This is how they can provoke those astonishing coincidences that sometimes play a key role even in a highly complex process like the development of a new production automobile.

Porsche Vision Turismo

年份: 2016
Year: 2016

研发状态: 1∶1硬质模型
Stage of development
Hard model, scale 1∶1

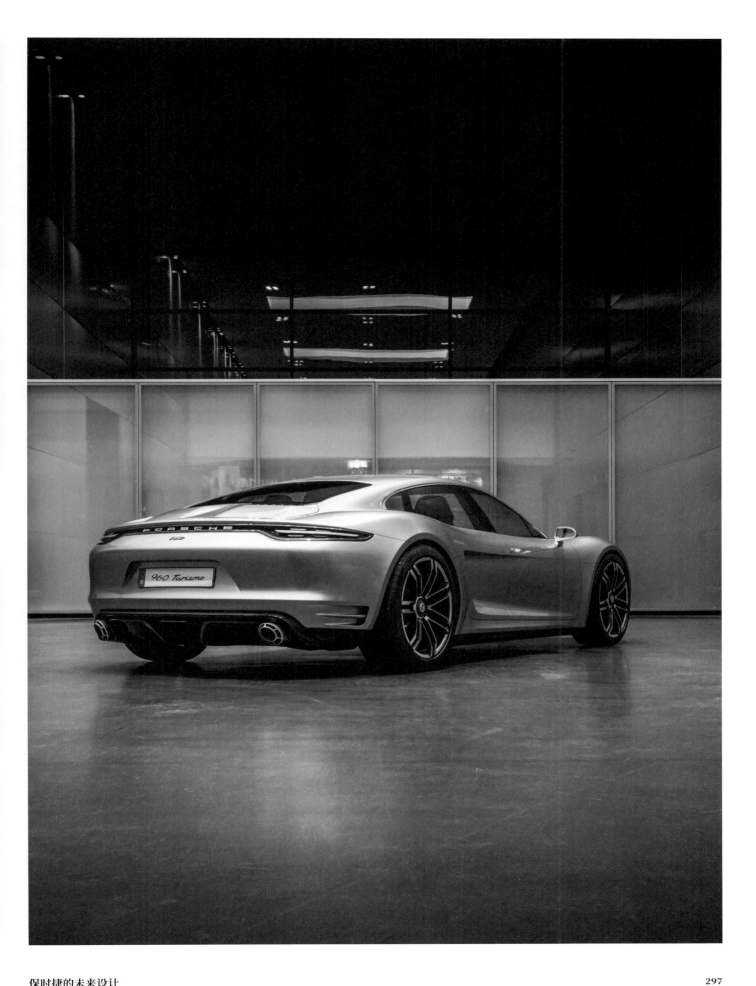

保时捷的未来设计

并非每个成功的系列车型的设计过程都简单直接。有时是一连串愉快的事故和意想不到的关联事物引导设计师迂回地实现了他的目标。保时捷品牌首款纯电动车 Taycan 就始于一场误会。"有一次在工作室里，我正路过一位设计师的画板，碰巧注意到一张保时捷918的草图，其中一条表示坡度的曲线被毡笔加粗强调了，"毛迈恪回忆道，"用我的余光看过去就像后门接缝的结构线。我很震惊！"

一款四座超级跑车的设想诞生了。现在的问题是找到合适的发动机来匹配特殊的运动比重：这辆新奇的跑车用中置发动机推动，还是追随品牌传统采用后置发动机——成为首款四座911？

"考虑到汽车电动化的比例和其持续增长的态势，我们发现使用纯电动驱动可以更有效地实现这一想法。"毛迈恪回忆道。这是四人座超级跑车发展成为保时捷 Taycan 的第一个进化阶段。

保时捷 Vision Turismo 还开创了新的造型趋势：后部带有保时捷标志的贯穿式灯带成为该品牌标识的永久性设计元素。如今，几乎所有保时捷车型上都可以找到它。电动车型的新设计标识也在前灯的基础上进一步发展和阐明。

Not every successful series model is the result of a straightforward design process. Sometimes it is a chain of happy accidents and unexpected constellations that lead a designer in a roundabout way to achieve his goal. The story of the Porsche Taycan, the brand's first ever fully-electric production sports car, began with a misunderstanding. "As I was passing one of our designers' drawing boards in our studio, I happened to notice a schematicdrawing of the Porsche 918. One line had been redrawn with a felt pen to emphasize the slope," remembers Michael Mauer. "Out of the corner of my eye it looked like a rear door joint. I was amazed!"

The idea of a Super Sports Car with four seats was born. Now the issue was to find the right engine to match the particularly sporty proportions: Could the adventurous sports car like this be propelled by a mid-engine? Or should it follow the brand's established tradition and have a rear engine – the first four-seater Porsche 911? "Taking account of the proportions and the emergence of electromobility, we found that the idea could be implemented even more effectively with a purely electric drive," recalls Michael Mauer. The four-seater Super Sports Car developed into the first evolutionary stage of the Porsche Taycan.

The Porsche Vision Turismo also set new trends in stylistic terms: the continuous light strip with the Porsche logo on the rear became a permanent fixture in the brand's identity. These days it is found in almost all models. The new design identity of the electric models was also further developed and defined on the basis of the front lights.

Porsche Vision "Renndienst"

年份: 2018
Year: 2018

研发状态: 1:1硬质模型
Stage of development
Hard model, scale 1:1

当专注于空间体验时，保时捷会是什么样子？这样的车能与现有的市场价值相协调吗？毛迈恪和他的团队在2018年以非比寻常的汽车愿景回答了这些问题。

保时捷 Vision "Renndienst"（"赛事服务"）是基于家用面包车的衍生版本，最多可容纳6人。在祖文豪森众多停着跑车的车库中都能发现它的身影。在保时捷品牌历史上甚至有它的前身：传奇的大众赛车服务车。然而，毛迈恪从一开始就很清楚，保时捷的大容量汽车不应该被定位和设计为无聊、实用的公共汽车，而是需要开辟新天地。因此，该团队设计了一款具有令人兴奋的比例的未来派"太空滑翔机"，以全新的方式将运动性与舒适性相结合。尽管如此，它从一开始就可以被认出是一辆保时捷。

带有平整车头的一体式铸造车身、强力张开的轮拱和不对称的车窗设计会让你忘记所有惯常的汽车类别。里面的乘客会发现这是个非常舒适、模块化的车厢。保时捷 Vision "Renndienst" 的驾驶员坐在一个居中的休息室式座椅上。单座布局提供了较为运动化的驾驶体验，也让后排乘客可以清楚地看到前方——在自动驾驶模式下，这种布局与传统的座椅排布相比，占用的空间更小。全电动驱动设备也紧凑地装填在车身底部。这使乘客能够拥有出乎意料的宽敞舒适的旅行体验。

当然，这款 Porsche Vision "Renndienst" 只是个设想，不过这样的实验性作品对保时捷来说也十分重要。它们有助于探索更多可能性并质疑既定的思维模式和惯例。这是"重新发明轮子"的唯一方法。

What might a Porsche look like when the focus is on the spatial experience? Can such a car be reconciled with existing market values? Michael Mauer and his team answered these questions in 2018 with an unusual automotive vision.

The Porsche Vision "Renndienst" ("Racing Service") is a loose variant of the family-friendly van for up to six people, which is already found in numerous garages parked next to a sports car from Zuffenhausen. It even has a predecessor in Porsche's brand history: the legendary VW Renndienst van. However, it was clear to Michael Mauer from the outset that a large-capacity automobile from Porsche should not be conceived and designed as a boring, practical bus, but instead needed to break new ground. And so the team designed a futuristic "spaceglider" with exciting proportions that combined sportiness with comfort in a completely new way. It is nevertheless recognizable as a Porsche right from the start.

The one-piece cast body with its flat front, the powerfully flared wheel arches and the asymmetrical window design make you forget all conventional categories. Inside passengers will find an extremely comfortable, modular interior cab. The driver of the Porsche Vision "Renndienst" sits on a central lounge-style seat. The single seat offers a sporty driving experience, allows passengers in the back a clear view to the front – and takes up less space in self-driving mode than a conventional row of seats. The fully electric drive technology is also compactly stowed in the underbody. This enables passengers to enjoy an unexpectedly spacious and comfortable travel experience.

Of course, the Porsche Vision "Renndienst" is just an idea. And yet such experimental visions are of essential importance for Porsche. They help in exploring options and in questioning established thought patterns and conventions. This is the only way to reinvent the wheel.

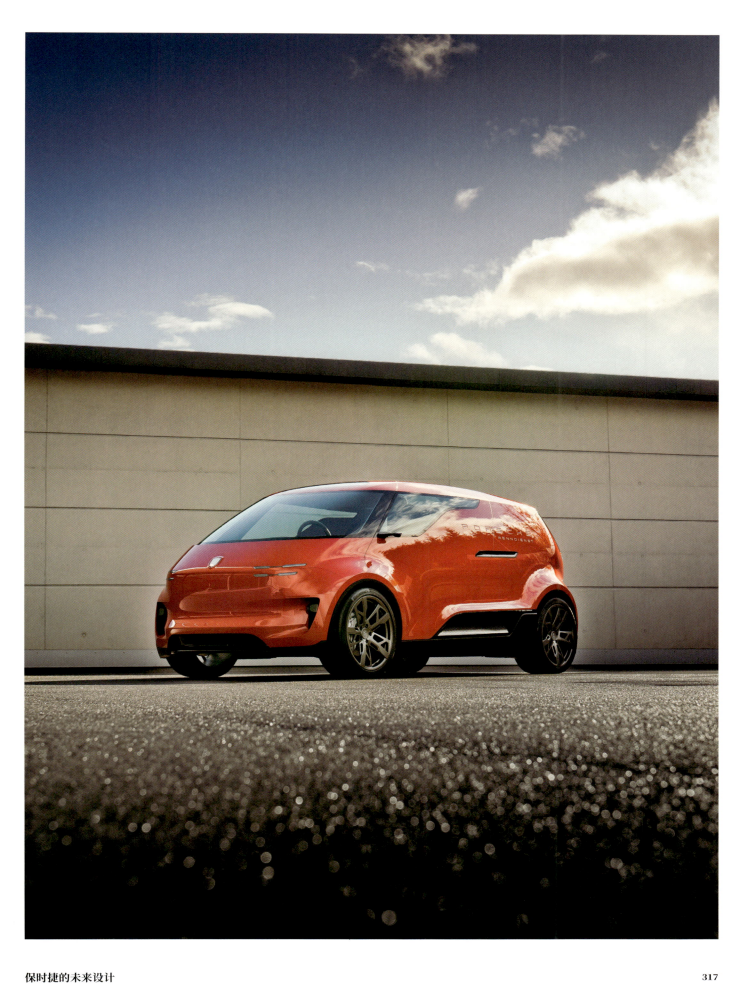

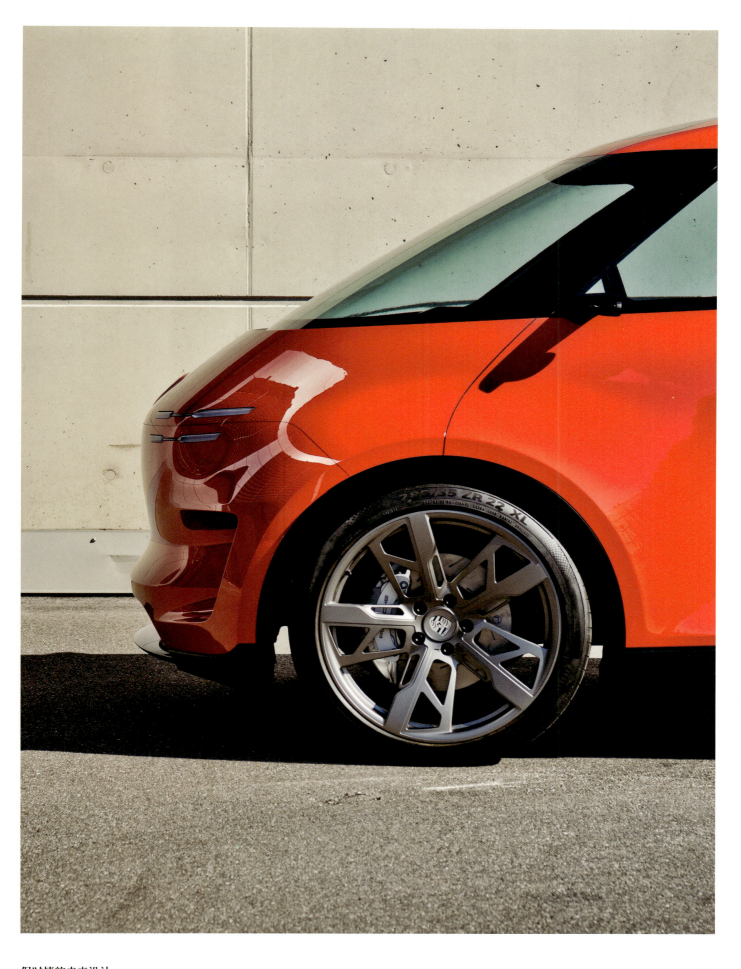

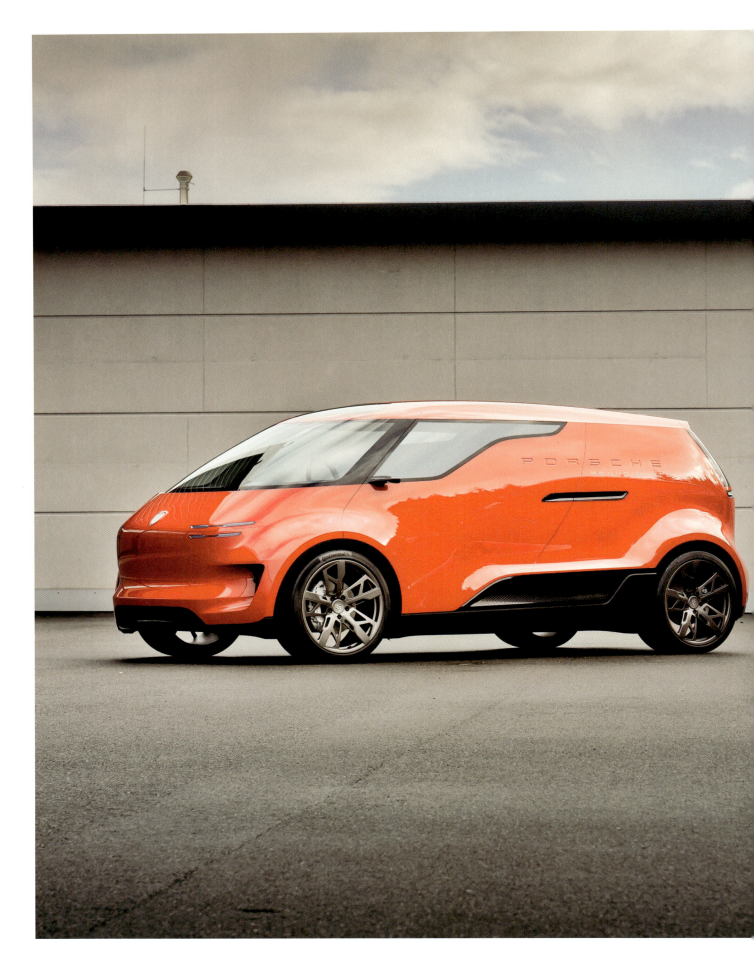

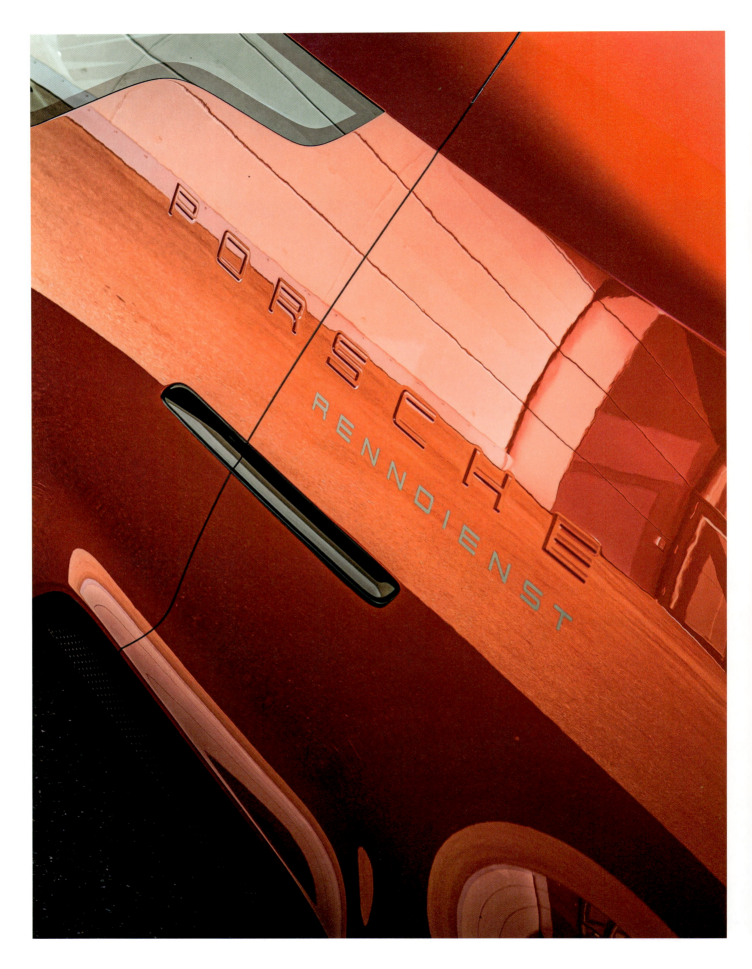

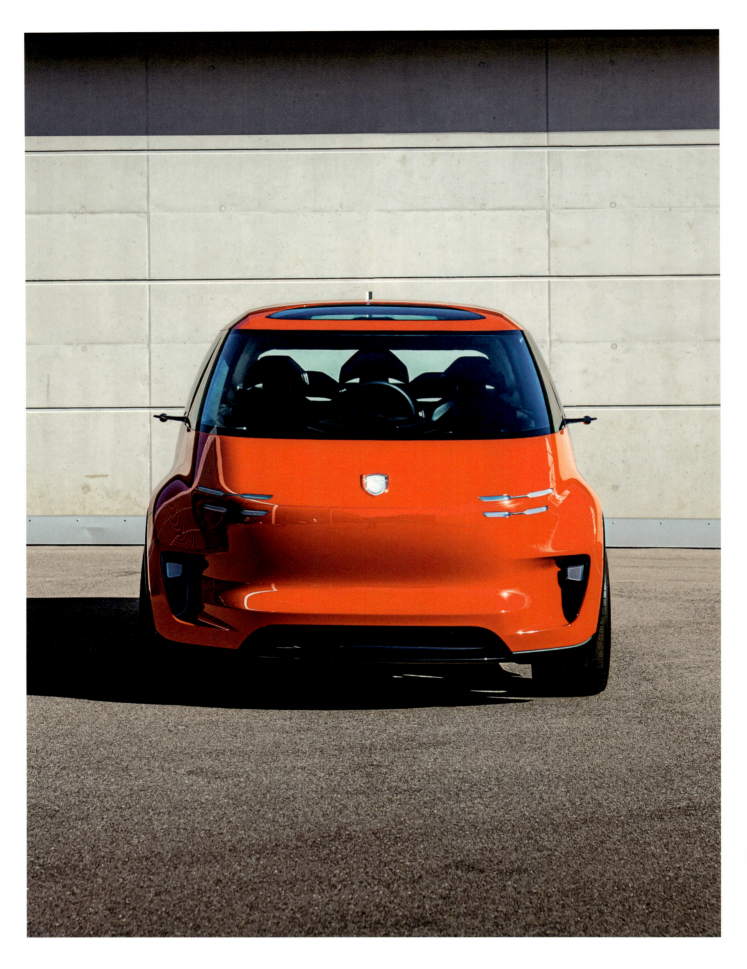

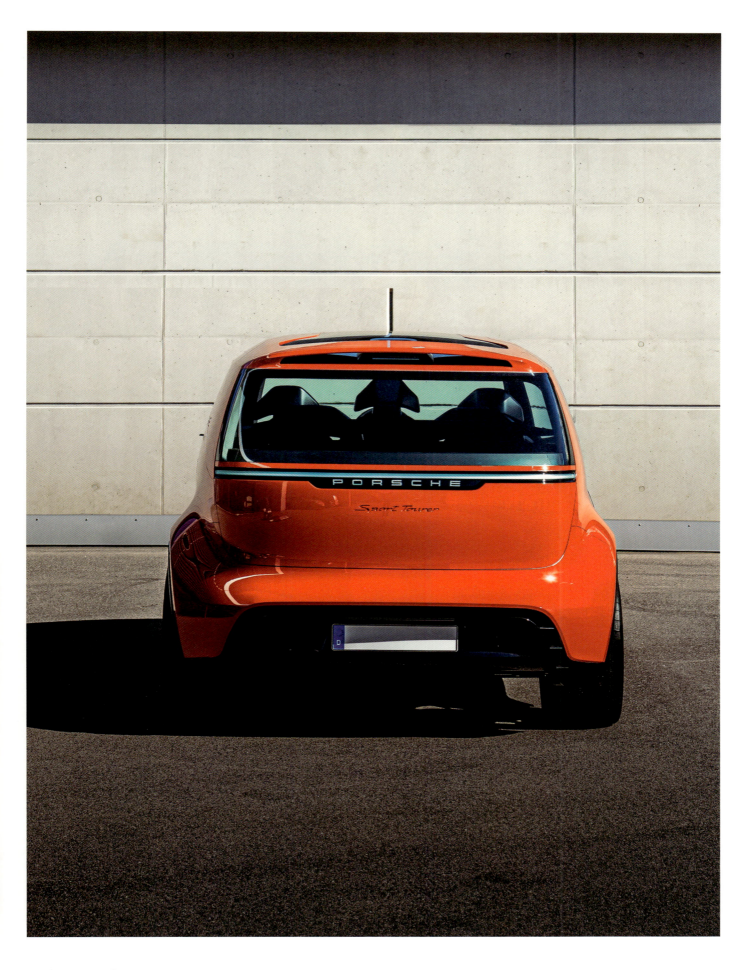

保时捷的未来设计

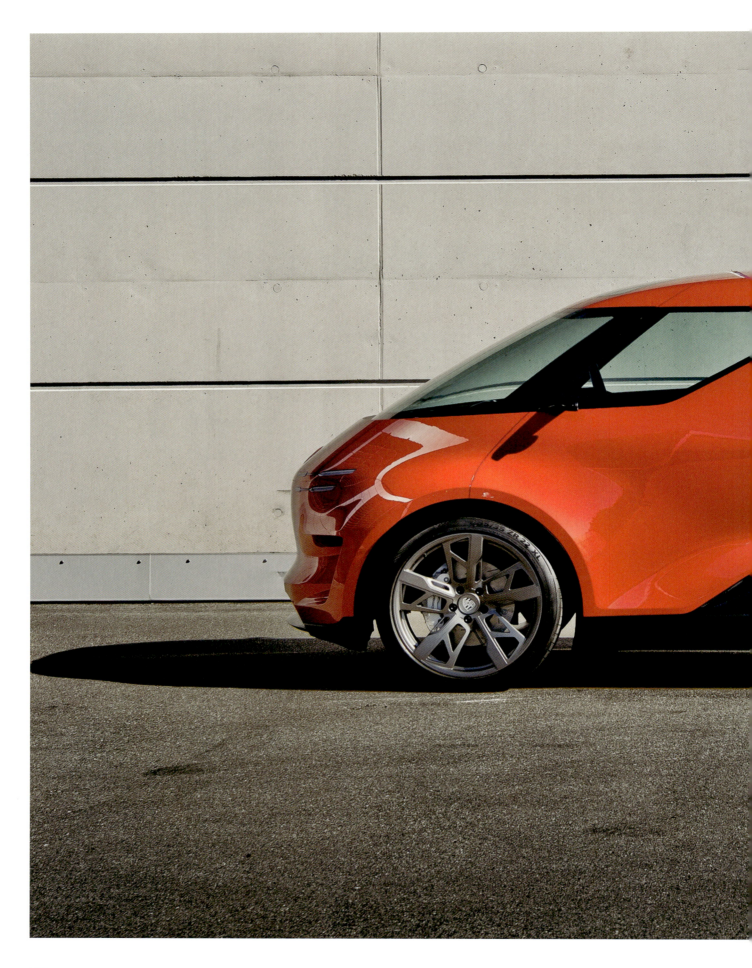

感谢公司内外的所有保时捷粉丝，他们全心全意地将保时捷打造成地球上最酷的汽车品牌。
Thanks go to all Porsche fans inside and outside the company who put their heart and soul into making Porsche the coolest car brand on the planet.

特别感谢奥博穆从一开始就对这个非凡项目的大力支持。因为他，这些愿景才得以重见天日。
Special thanks to Oliver Blume for his enormous enthusiasm in supporting this extraordinary project from the outset. It is due to him that these visions have seen the light of day.

创意：毛迈恪
Idea: Michael Mauer

概念：斯特凡·博格纳
Concept: Stefan Bogner

文字：扬·卡尔·贝德克尔
Text: Jan Karl Baedeker

版式：斯特凡·博格纳
Layout: Stefan Bogner

摄影：斯特凡·博格纳
Photography: Stefan Bogner

翻译：丁伯骏，詹姆斯·奥尼尔
Translation: Ding Bojun, James O'Neill

湖 岸
Hu'an *publications*®

出版统筹 _ 唐　奂

联合出品 _ 保时捷中国　《驾道 drivestyle》

策划编辑 _ 景　雁

特约编辑 _ 周　赟

责任编辑 _ 张雅洁

美术编辑 _ 陆宣其

营销编辑 _ 王翔宇

🐦 @huan404
微博 湖岸 Huan
www.huan404.com
联系电话 _ 010-87923806
投稿邮箱 _ info@huan404.com

感谢您选择一本湖岸的书
欢迎关注"湖岸"微信公众号